EGYPTIAN MYTHS AND LEGENDS

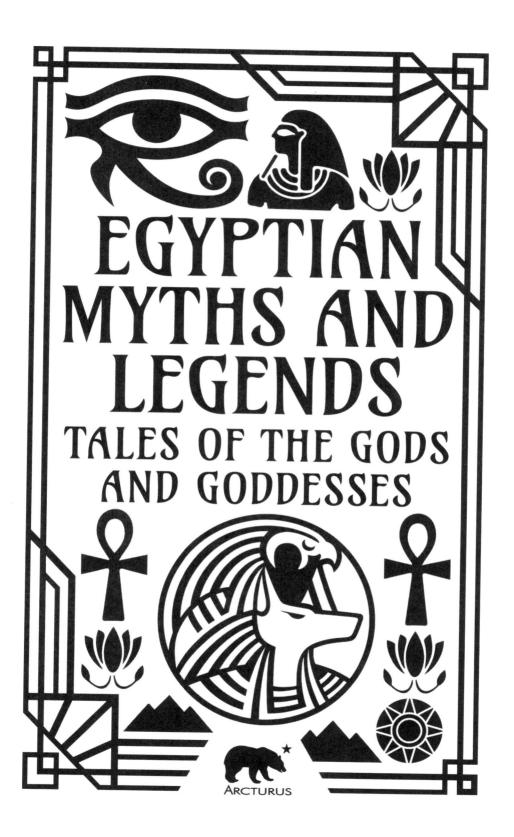

EGYPTIAN MYTHS AND LEGENDS

TALES OF THE GODS AND GODDESSES

ARCTURUS

DISCLAIMER

Throughout the text readers may find that some
of the language used and sentiments expressed are
offensive and unacceptable by today's standards.
These reflect the attitudes and usage common at
the time the book was written. In no way do they
reflect the attitude of the publishers.

ARCTURUS

This edition published in 2024 by Arcturus Publishing Limited
26/27 Bickels Yard, 151–153 Bermondsey Street,
London SE1 3HA

ISBN: 978-1-3988-4609-8
AD012242UK

Printed in China

CONTENTS

INTRODUCTION

S ir Ernest Alfred Thompson Wallis Budge was born in Cornwall in 1857. Before long, he moved to London to live with his maternal aunt and grandmother. In 1869, he left school at age twelve to clerk for W.H. Smith but spent every free moment pursuing his passion for languages, fascinated particularly with Hebrew and Syriac. Budge's fervent study quickly drew the attention of his employer, W.H. Smith, who recognized the boy's promise and raised money to send him to Cambridge University, where he would study from 1878 to 1883.

What followed was an illustrious career in ancient languages and cultures. In 1883, Budge entered the British Museum's Department of Egyptian and Assyrian Antiquities, travelling to Egypt and Iraq to acquire cuneiform tablets, ancient manuscripts, and hieroglyphic papyri, contributing greatly to the Museum's extensive collection. He continued to climb the British Museum's hierarchy, ultimately becoming Keeper in his department in 1894. All the while, Budge, a prolific author, produced several publications on Egyptian religion and myths. He was knighted in 1920 for his contributions to Egyptology, and since his death

in 1934, his work has remained consistently in print, just as influential as ever.

Sir William Matthew Flinders Petrie was born in Kent in 1853 to William Petrie and Anne Flinders. William, an electrical engineer, and Anne, daughter of famed British explorer Captain Matthew Flinders, educated their son at home. Though he would never receive formal education, his expansive mental capacity was obvious from a young age. As a teenager, he surveyed British prehistoric monuments, producing the era's most accurate survey of Stonehenge.

Upon travelling to Giza in 1880, Petrie grew disappointed with the rapid deterioration of Egyptian monuments and sought to preserve them through writing. He was offered a position in Egyptology with University College London, which funded his excavations in Egypt. He would, throughout his career, play an instrumental role in the Tanis dig (1884), the Tell Nebesheh dig (1886), and the unearthing of the temple of Aten in Amarna (1891), as well as several other historically significant archaeological undertakings. He was knighted in 1923 before shifting his work's focus to Palestine, which would occupy his time until his death in 1942. On top of mythological writings and accounts of historical sites, he left behind an entirely new, more efficient excavation method still used today.

Though Petrie and Budge were professional enemies due to their conflicting views on the origins of Egyptian religion, their bodies of translative work interweave seamlessly to create a stunning tapestry of Ancient Egyptian culture and beliefs.

Some of their most exceptional translations are collected here in *Egyptian Myths and Legends*. Within its pages, we are given insight into the Creation myth, the God-king Ra's fear of reptiles, the undying generational leadership of Horus, the terrible famine born of Khnemu's wrath, the wonderful exploits of three magicians, and the famous tale of Apnu and Bata, as well as many other enlightening myths. This collection also contains, alongside the works of Petrie and Budge, the incomplete yet magnificent story of Setna, edited and translated by Lewis Spence, a Scottish myth and folklore expert.

Together, these stories amalgamate to reveal the values, beliefs, and culture of Ancient Egypt. Beyond educationally enlightening, these gripping tales told with the unique Egyptian prowess for narrative are an absolute treat to read.

THE LITERATURE AND MYTHOLOGY OF ANCIENT EGYPT

E. A. Wallis Budge and W. M. Flinders Petrie

The literature of ancient Egypt is the product of a period of about four thousand years, and it was written in three kinds of writing, which are called hieroglyphic, hieratic, and demotic. In the first of these the characters were pictures of objects, in the second the forms of the characters were made as simple as possible so that they might be written quickly, and in the third many of them lost their picture form altogether and became mere symbols. Egyptian writing was believed to have been invented by the god Tehuti, or Thoth, and as this god was thought to be a form of the mind and intellect and wisdom of the God who created the heavens and the earth, the picture characters, or hieroglyphs as they are called, were held to be holy, or divine, or sacred. Certain religious texts were thought to possess special virtue when written in hieroglyphs, and the chapters and sections of books that were considered to have been composed by Thoth himself were believed to possess very great power, and to be of the utmost benefit to the dead when they were written out for them in hieroglyphs, and buried with them in their coffins. Thoth also invented the science of numbers, and as he fixed the courses of the sun, moon, and stars, and ordered the seasons, he was thought to be the first astronomer. He was the lord of wisdom, and the possessor of all knowledge, both heavenly and earthly, divine and human; and he was the author of every attempt made by man to draw, paint, and carve. As the lord and maker of books, and as the skilled scribe, he was the clerk of the gods, and kept the registers wherein the deeds of men were written down. The deep knowledge of Thoth enabled him to find out the truth at all times, and this ability caused the Egyptians to assign to him the position of Chief Judge of the dead. A very ancient legend states that Thoth acted in this capacity in the great trial that took place in heaven when Osiris was accused of certain crimes by his twin-brother Set, the god of evil. Thoth examined the evidence, and proved to the gods that the charges made by Set were untrue, and that Osiris had spoken the truth and that Set was a liar. For this reason every Egyptian prayed that Thoth might act for him as he did for Osiris, and that on the day of the Great Judgment Thoth might preside over the weighing of his heart in the Balance. All the important religious works in all periods were believed to have been composed either by himself, or by holy scribes who were inspired by him. They were believed to be sources of the deepest wisdom, the like of which existed in no other books in the world.

At a very early period the Egyptians learned how to make a sort of paper, which is now universally known by the name of 'papyrus'. When they made this discovery cannot be said, but the hieroglyphic inscriptions of the early dynasties contain the picture of a roll of papyrus, and the antiquity of the use of papyrus must therefore be very great. Among the oldest dated examples of inscribed papyrus may be noted some accounts which were written in the reign of King Assa (fourth dynasty, 3400 BC), and which were found at Sakkārah, about 20 miles (32 km) to the south of Cairo. Papyrus was made from the papyrus plant that grew and flourished in the swamps and marshes of Lower Egypt, and in the shallow pools that were formed by the annual Nile flood. the Egyptians made their paper from it by cutting the inner part of the stem into thin strips, the width of which depended upon the thickness of the stem; the length of these varied, of course, with the length of the stem. To make a sheet of papyrus several of these strips were laid side by side lengthwise, and several others were laid over them crosswise. Thus each sheet of papyrus contained two layers, which were joined together by means of glue and water or gum.

THE EGYPTIAN STORY OF CREATION

If we consider for a moment the vast amount of thought which the Egyptian gave to the problems of the future life, and his deep-seated belief in resurrection and immortality, we cannot fail to conclude that he must have theorized deeply about the constitution of the heaven in which he hoped to live everlastingly, and about its Maker. The translations given in the following pages prove that the theologians of Egypt were ready enough to describe heaven, and the life led by the blessed there, and the powers and the attributes of the gods, but they appear to have shrunk from writing down in a connected form their beliefs concerning the Creation and the origin of the Creator. The worshippers of each great god proclaimed him to be the Creator of All, and every great town had its own local belief on the subject. According to the Heliopolitans, Atem, or Tem, and at a later period Ra, was the Creator; according to Memphite theology he was Ptah; according to the Hermopolitans he was Thoth; and according to the Thebans he was Amen (Ammon). In only one native Egyptian work up to the present has there been discovered any connected account of the Creation, and the means by which it was effected, namely, the British Museum Papyrus, No. 10,188. This papyrus was written about 305 BC, and is therefore of a comparatively late date, but the subject matter of the works contained in it is thousands of years older, and it is only their forms which are of a late date. The Story of the Creation is found in the last work in the papyrus, which is called the 'Book of overthrowing Āapep, the Enemy of Ra, the Enemy of Un-Nefer' (i.e. Osiris). This work is a liturgy, which was said at certain times of the day and night in the great temple of Amen-Ra at Thebes, with the view of preventing the monster Āapep from obstructing the sunrise. Āapep was supposed to lie in wait for the sun daily just before sunrise, with the view of doing battle with him and overthrowing him. When the Sun-god arrived at the place where Āapep was, he first of all cast a spell upon the monster, which rendered him helpless, and then he cast his fiery rays upon him, which shrivelled him up, and the fire of the god consumed him entirely. In the temple of Amen-Ra the priests recited the spells that were supposed to help the Sun-god to burn up Āapep, and they burnt waxen figures of the monster in specially prepared fires, and, uttering curses, they trampled them under foot and defiled them. These spells and burnings were also believed to break up rain clouds, and to scatter fog and mist and to dissipate thunder-storms, and to help the sun to rise on this world in a cloudless sky. Āapep was a form of Set, the god of evil of every kind, and his allies were the 'Red Fiends' and the 'Black Fiends', and every power of darkness. In the midst of the magical spells of this papyrus we find two copies of the 'Book of knowing how Ra came into being, and of overthrowing Āapep.' One copy is a little fuller than the other, but they agree substantially. The words of this book are said in the opening line to have been spoken by the god Nebertcher, i.e. the 'Lord to the uttermost limit,' or God Himself. The Egyptian Christians, or Copts, in their religious writings use this name as an equivalent of God Almighty, the Lord of All, the God of the Universe. Nebertcher says: 'I am the creator of what hath come into being. I myself came into being under the form of the god Khepera. I came into being under the form of Pautti (or, in primeval time), I formed myself out of the primeval matter, I made myself out of the substance that was in primeval time.' Nothing existed at that time except the great primeval watery mass called Nu, but in this there were the germs of everything that came into being subsequently. There was no heaven, and no earth, and the god found no place on which to stand; nothing, in fact, existed except the god. He says, 'I was alone.' He first created himself by uttering his own name as a word of power, and when this was uttered his visible form appeared. He then uttered another kind of word of power, and as a result of this his soul (ba) came into being, and it worked in connection with his heart or mind (ab). Before every act of creation Nebertcher, or his visible form Khepera, thought out what form the thing to be created was to take, and when he had uttered its name the thing itself appeared in heaven or earth. To fill the heaven, or place where he lived, the god next produced from his body and its shadow the two gods Shu and Tefnut. These with Nebertcher, or Khepera, formed the first triad of gods, and the 'one god became three', or, as we should say, the one god had three aspects, each of which was quite distinct from the other. The tradition of the begetting of Shu and Tefnut is as old as the time of the pyramids, for it is mentioned in the text of Pepi I, l. 466. The next act of creation resulted in the emerging of the Eye of Nebertcher (later identified with Ra) from the watery mass (Nu), and light shone upon its waters. Shu and Tefnut then united and they produced Keb, the Earth-god, and Nut, the Sky-goddess. The text then refers to some calamity which befell the Eye of Nebertcher or of Khepera, but what it was is not clear; at all events the Eye became obscured, and it ceased to give light. This period of darkness is, of course, the night, and to obviate the inconvenience caused by this recurring period of darkness, the god made a second Eye, i.e. the moon, and set it in the heavens. The greater Eye ruled the day, and the lesser Eye the night. One of the results of the daily darkness was the descent of the Sky-goddess Nut to the Earth-god Keb each evening.

The gods and goddesses next created were five, namely, Osiris, Horus, Set, Isis, and Nephthys. Osiris married Isis, and their son was called Horus; Set married Nephthys, but their son Anpu, or Anubis, is not mentioned in our text. Osiris became the great Ancestor-god of Egypt, and was a reincarnation of his great-grandfather. Men and women were first formed from the tears that fell from the Eye of Khepera, or the Sun-god, upon his body; the old Egyptian word for 'men' very closely resembles in form and sound the word for 'tears'. Plants, vegetables, herbs, and trees owe their origin to the light of the moon falling upon the earth. Our text contains no mention of a special creation of the 'beasts of the field', but the god states distinctly that he created the children of the earth, or creeping things of all kinds, and among this class quadrupeds are probably included. The men and women, and all the other living creatures that were made at that time by Nebertcher, or Khepera, reproduced their species, each in his own way, and thus the earth became filled with their descendants as we see at the present time. The elements of this Creation legend are very, very old, and the form in which they are grouped in our text suggests the influence of the priests of Heliopolis. It is interesting to note that only very ancient gods appear as Powers of creation, and these were certainly worshipped for many centuries before the priests of Heliopolis invented their cult of the Sun-god, and identified their god with the older gods of the country. We may

note, too, that gods like Ptah and Amen, whose reputation was so great in later times, and even when our text was copied in 305 BC, find no mention at all.

LEGENDS OF THE GODS

The Egyptians believed that at one time all the great gods and goddesses lived upon earth, and that they ruled Egypt in much the same way as the Pharaohs with whom they were more or less acquainted. They went about among men and took a real personal interest in their affairs, and, according to tradition, they spared no pains in promoting their wishes and well-being. Their rule was on the whole beneficent, chiefly because in addition to their divine attributes they possessed natures, and apparently bodily constitutions that were similar to those of men. Like men also they were supposed to feel emotions and passions, and to be liable to the accidents that befell men, and to grow old, and even to die. The greatest of all the gods was Ra, and he reigned over Egypt for very many years. His reign was marked by justice and righteousness, and he was in all periods of Egyptian history regarded as the type of what a king should be. When men instead of gods reigned over Egypt they all delighted to call themselves sons of Ra, and every king believed that Ra was his true father, and regarded his mother's husband as his father only in name. This belief was always common in Egypt, and even Alexander the Great found it expedient to adopt it, for he made a journey to the sanctuary of Amen (Ammon) in the Oasis of Sīwāh in order to be officially acknowledged by the god. Having obtained this recognition, he became the rightful lord of Egypt.

EGYPTIAN TALES

It seems that any simple form of fiction is supposed to be a 'fairy tale': which implies that it has to do with an impossible world of imaginary beings. Now the Egyptian Tales are exactly the opposite of this, as they relate the doings and the thoughts of men and women who are human. Whatever there is of supernatural elements is a very part of the beliefs and motives of the people whose lives are here pictured. But most of what is here might happen in some corner of our own country to-day, where ancient beliefs may have a home. So far, then, from being fairy tales there is not a single being that could be termed a fairy in the whole of them.

The real and genuine charm of all fiction is that of enabling the reader to place himself in the mental position of another, to see with the eyes, to feel with the thoughts, to reason with the mind, of a wholly different being. All the greatest work has this charm. It may be to place the reader in new mental positions, or in a different level of the society that he already knows, either higher or lower; or it may be to make alive to him a society of a different land or age. It is the transplanting of the reader into a new life, the doubling of his mental experience, that is the very power of fiction. The same

interest attaches to these tales. In place of regarding Egyptians only as the builders of pyramids and the makers of mummies, we here see the men and women as they lived, their passions, their foibles, their beliefs, and their follies. The old refugee Sanehat craving to be buried with his ancestors in the blessed land, the enterprise and success of the Doomed Prince, the sweetness of Bata, the misfortunes of Ahura – these all live before us, and we can for a brief half hour share the feelings and see with the eyes of those who ruled the world when it was young. This is the real value of these tales, and the power which still belongs to the oldest literature in the world. The earliest is purely a collection of marvels or fabulous incidents of the simplest kind. Then we advance to contrasts between town and country, between Egypt and foreign lands. Then personal adventure, and the interest in schemes and successes, becomes the staple material; while only in the later periods does character come in as the groundwork.

A NOTE ON TRANSLATION

The specimens of native Egyptian Literature printed herein are taken from tombs, papyri, stelæ, and other monuments, and, with few exceptions, each specimen is complete in itself. Translations of most of the texts have appeared in learned works written by Egyptologists in English, French, German, and Italian, but some appear in English for the first time. In every case I have collated my own translations with the texts, and, thanks to the accurate editions of texts which have appeared in recent years, it has been found possible to make many hitherto difficult passages clear. The translations are as literal as the difference between the Egyptian and English idioms will permit, but it has been necessary to insert particles and often to invert the order of the words in the original works in order to produce a connected meaning in English. The result of this has been in many cases to break up the short abrupt sentences in which the Egyptian author delighted, and which he used frequently with dramatic effect. Extraordinarily concise phrases have been

paraphrased, but the meanings given to several unknown words often represent guess-work.

E. A. Wallis Budge

In translating these documents into English I have freely used the various translations already published in other languages; but in all cases more or less revision and retranslation from the original has been made. In this matter I am indebted to Mr F. Ll. Griffith, who has in some cases – as in Anpu and Bata – almost entirely retranslated the original papyrus. As to the actual phraseology, I am alone responsible for that. How far original idiom should be retained in any translation is always a debated question, and must entirely depend on the object in view. Here the purpose of rendering the work intelligible to ordinary readers required the modifying of some idioms and the paraphrasing of others. But so far as possible the style and tone of the original has been preserved, and whatever could be easily followed has been left to speak for itself.

W. M. Flinders Petrie

THE LEGEND OF THE GOD NEBERTCHER, AND THE HISTORY OF CREATION

The text of the remarkable Legend of the Creation which forms the first section of this volume is preserved in a well-written papyrus in the British Museum, where it bears the number 10,188. This papyrus was acquired by the late Mr A. H. Rhind in 1861 or 1862, when he was excavating some tombs on the west bank of the Nile at Thebes. The text is written in a small, very black, but neat hand, and may be assigned to a time between the XXVIth Dynasty and the Ptolemaic Period. This curious 'book' describes the origin not only of heaven, and earth, and all therein, but also of God Himself.

The words which the god Nebertcher spake after he had come into being: – 'I am he who came into being in the form of the god Khepera, and I am the creator of that which came into being, that is to say, I am the creator of everything which came into being: now the things which I created, and which came forth out of my mouth after that I had come into being myself were exceedingly many. The sky (or heaven) had not come into being, the earth did not exist, and the children of the earth, and the creeping, things, had not been made at that time. I myself raised them up from out of Nu, from a state of helpless inertness. I found no place whereon I could stand. I worked a charm upon my own heart (or, will), I laid the foundation [of things] by Maat, and I made everything which had form. I was [then] one by myself, for I had not emitted from myself the god Shu, and I had not spit out from myself the goddess Tefnut; and there existed no other who could work with me. I laid the foundations [of things] in my own heart, and there came into being multitudes of created things, which came into being from the created things which were born from the created things which arose from what they brought forth. I had union with my closed hand, and I embraced my shadow as a wife, and I poured seed into my own mouth, and I sent forth from myself issue in the form of the gods Shu and Tefnut. Saith my father Nu: – My Eye was covered up behind them (i.e., Shu and Tefnut), but after two hen periods had passed from the time when they departed from me, from being one god I became three gods, and I came into being in the earth. Then Shu and Tefnut rejoiced from out of the inert watery mass wherein they I were, and they brought to me my Eye (i.e., the sun). Now after these things I gathered together my members, and I wept over them, and men and women sprang into being from the tears which came forth from my Eye. And when my Eye came to me, and found that I had made another [Eye] in place where it was (i.e., the moon), it was wroth with (or, raged at) me, whereupon I endowed it (i.e., the second Eye) with [some of] the splendour which I had made for the first [Eye], and I made it to occupy its place in my Face, and henceforth it ruled throughout all this earth.'

'When there fell on them their moment through plant-like clouds, I restored what had been taken away from them, and I appeared from out of the plant-like clouds. I created creeping things of every kind, and everything which came into being from them. Shu and Tefnut brought forth [Seb and] Nut; and Seb and Nut brought forth Osiris, and Heru-khent-an-maati, and Set, and Isis, and Nephthys at one birth, one after the other, and they produced their multitudinous offspring in this earth.'

THE DESTRUCTION OF MANKIND

Translated by E. A. Wallis Budge

The text containing the Legend of the Destruction of Mankind is written in hieroglyphs, and is found on the four walls of a small chamber which is entered from the 'hall of columns' in the tomb of Seti I, which is situated on the west bank of the Nile at Thebes. On the wall facing the door of this chamber is painted in red the figure of the large 'Cow of Heaven'. The lower part of her belly is decorated with a series of thirteen stars, and immediately beneath it are the two Boats of Ra, called Semketet and Mantchet, or Sektet and Matet. Each of her four legs is held in position by two gods, and the god Shu, with outstretched uplifted arms, supports her body. The legend takes us back to the time when the gods of Egypt went about in the country, and mingled with men and were thoroughly acquainted with their desires and needs.

CHAPTER I

[ere is the story of Ra,] the god who was self-begotten and self-created, after he had assumed the sovereignty over men and women, and gods, and things, the ONE god. Now men and women were speaking words of complaint, saying: – 'Behold, his Majesty (Life, Strength, and Health to him!) hath grown old, and his bones have become like silver, and his members have turned into gold and his hair is like unto real lapis-lazuli.' His Majesty heard the words of complaint which men and women were uttering, and his Majesty (Life, Strength, and Health to him!) said unto those who were in his train: – 'Cry out, and bring to me my Eye, and Shu, and Tefnut, and Seb, and Nut, and the father-gods, and the mother-gods who were with me, even when I was in Nu side by side with my god Nu. Let there be brought along with my Eye his ministers, and let them be led to me hither secretly, so that men and women may not perceive them [coming] hither, and may not therefore take to flight with their hearts. Come thou with them to the Great House, and let them declare their plans (or, arrangements) fully, for I will go from Nu into the place wherein I brought about my own existence, and let those gods be brought unto me there.' Now the gods were drawn up on each side of Ra, and they bowed down before his Majesty until their heads touched the ground, and the maker of men and women, the king of those who have knowledge, spake his words in the presence of the Father of the first-born gods. And the gods spake in the presence of his Majesty, saying: – 'Speak unto us, for we are listening to them' (i.e., thy words). Then Ra spake unto Nu, saying: – 'O thou first-born god from whom I came into being, O ye gods of ancient time, my ancestors, take ye heed to what men and women [are doing]; for behold, those who were created by my Eye are uttering words of complaint against me. Tell me what ye would do in the matter, and consider this thing for me, and seek out [a plan] for me, for I will not slay them until I have heard what ye shall say to me concerning it.'

Then the Majesty of Nu, to son Ra, spake, saying: – 'Thou art the god who art greater than he who made thee, thou art the sovereign of those who were created with thee, thy throne is set, and the fear of thee is great; let thine Eye go against those who have uttered blasphemies against thee.' And the Majesty of Ra, said: – 'Behold, they have betaken themselves to flight into the mountain lands, for their hearts are afraid because of the words which they have uttered.' Then the gods spake in the presence of his Majesty, saying: – 'Let thine Eye go forth and let it destroy for thee those who revile thee with words of evil, for there is no eye whatsoever that can go before it and resist thee and it when it journeyeth in the form of Hathor.' Thereupon this goddess went forth and slew the men and the women who were on the mountain (or, desert land). And the Majesty of this god said, 'Come, come in peace, O Hathor, for the work is accomplished.' Then this goddess said, 'Thou hast made me to live, for when I gained the mastery over men and women it was sweet to my heart;' and the Majesty of Ra said, 'I myself will be master over them as [their] king, and I will destroy them.' And it came to pass that Sekhet of the offerings

waded about in the night season in their blood, beginning at
Suten-henen. Then the Majesty of Ra, spake [saying], 'Cry out,
and let there come to me swift and speedy messengers who shall
be able to run like the wind . . .;' and straightway messengers of
this kind were brought unto him. And the Majesty of this god
spake [saying], 'Let these messengers go to Abu, and bring unto
me mandrakes in great numbers;' and [when] these mandrakes
were brought unto him the Majesty of this god gave them to
Sekhet, the goddess who dwelleth in Annu (Heliopolis) to crush.
And behold, when the maidservants were bruising the grain for
[making] beer, these mandrakes were placed in the vessels which
were to hold the beer, and some of the blood of the men and
women [who had been slain]. Now they made seven thousand
vessels of beer. Now when the Majesty of Re, the King of the
South and North, had come with the gods to look at the vessels
of beer, and behold, the daylight had appeared after the slaughter
of men and women by the goddess in their season as she sailed up
the river, the Majesty of Ra said, 'It is good, it is good, nevertheless
I must protect men and women against her.' And Ra said, 'Let
them take up the vases and carry them to the place where the
men and women were slaughtered by her.' Then the Majesty of the
King of the South and North in the three-fold beauty of the night
caused to be poured out these vases of beer which make [men] to
lie down (or, sleep), and the meadows of the Four Heavens were
filled with beer (or, water) by reason of the Souls of the Majesty
of this god. And it came to pass that when this goddess arrived
at the dawn of day, she found these [Heavens] flooded [with

beer], and she was pleased thereat; and she drank [of the beer and blood], and her heart rejoiced, and she became drunk, and she gave no further attention to men and women. Then said the Majesty of Ra to this goddess, 'Come in peace, come in peace, O Amit,' and thereupon beautiful women came into being in the city of Amit (or, Amem). And the Majesty of Ra spake [concerning] this goddess, [saying], 'Let there be made for her vessels of the beer which produceth sleep at every holy time and season of the year, and they shall be in number according to the number of my hand-maidens;' and from that early time until now men have been wont to make on the occasions of the festival of Hathor vessels of the beer which make them to sleep in number according to the number of the handmaidens of Ra. And the Majesty of Ra spake unto this goddess, [saying], 'I am smitten with the pain of the fire of sickness; whence cometh to me [this] pain?' And the Majesty of Ra said, 'I live, but my heart hath become exceedingly weary with existence with them (i.e., with men); I have slain [some of] them, but there is a remnant of worthless ones, for the destruction which I wrought among them was not as great as my power.' Then the gods who were in his following said unto him, 'Be not overcome by thy inactivity, for thy might is in proportion to thy will.' And the Majesty of this god said unto the Majesty of Nu, 'My members are weak for (or, as at) the first time; I will not permit this to come upon me a second time.' And the Majesty of the god Nu said, 'O son Shu, be thou the Eye 'for thy father . . . and avenue (?) him, and 'thou goddess Nut, place him . . . And the goddess Nut said, 'How can this be then, O my father Nu?

Hail,' said Nut . . . to the god Nu, and the goddess straightway became [a cow], and she set the Majesty of Ra upon [her] back . . . And when these things had been done, men and women saw the god Ra, upon the back [of the cow]. Then these men and women said, 'Remain with us, and we will overthrow thine enemies who speak words of blasphemy [against thee], and [destroy them].' Then his Majesty [Ra] set out for the Great House, and [the gods who were in the train of Ra remained] with them (i.e., the men); during that time the earth was in darkness. And when the earth became light [again] and the morning had dawned, the men came forth with their bows and their [weapons], and they set their arms in motion to shoot the enemies [of Ra]. Then said the Majesty of this god, 'Your transgressions of violence are placed behind you, for the slaughtering of the enemies is above the slaughter [of sacrifice];' thus came into being the slaughter [of sacrifice]. And the Majesty of this god said unto Nut, 'I have placed myself upon my back in order to stretch myself out.' What then is the meaning of this? It meaneth that he united (?) himself with Nut. [Thus came into being] . . . Then said the Majesty of this god, 'I am departing from them (i.e., from men), and he must come after me who would see me;' thus came into being . . . Then the Majesty of this god looked forth from its interior, saying, 'Gather together [men for me], and make ready for me an abode for multitudes;' thus came into being . . . And his Majesty (life, health, and strength be to him!) said, 'Let a great field (sekhet) be produced (hetep);' thereupon Sekhet-hetep came into being. [And the god said], 'I will gather herbs (aarat) therein;' thereupon Sekhet-aaru came into being.

[And the god said], 'I will make it to contain as dwellers things (khet) like stars of all sorts;' thereupon the stars (akhekha) came into being. Then the goddess Nut trembled because of the height.

And the Majesty of Ra said, 'I decree that supports be to bear [the goddess up];' thereupon the props of heaven (heh) came into being. And the Majesty of Ra said, 'O my son Shu, I pray thee to set thyself under [my] daughter Nut, and guard thou for me the supports (heh) of the millions (heh) which are there, and which live in darkness. Take thou the goddess upon thy head, and act thou as nurse for her;' thereupon came into being [the custom] of a son nursing a daughter, and [the custom] of a father carrying a son upon his head.

CHAPTER II

This Chapter shall be said over [a figure of] the cow. – The supporters [called] Heh-enti shall be by her shoulder. The supporters [called] Heh-enti shall be at her side, and one cubit and four spans of hers shall be in colours, and nine stars shall be on her belly, and Set shall be by her two thighs and shall keep watch before her two legs, and before her two legs shall be Shu, under her belly, and he shall be made (i.e., painted) in green qenat colour. His two arms shall be under the stars, and his name shall be made (i.e., written) in the middle of them, namely, Shu himself. 'A boat with a rudder and a double shrine shall be therein, and Aten (i.e., the Disk) shall be above it, and Ra shall be in it, in front of Shu, near his hand, or, as another reading hath, behind him, near his hand. And the udders of the Cow shall be made to be between her legs, towards the left side. And on the two flanks, towards the middle of the legs, shall be done in writing [the words], 'The exterior heaven,' and 'I am what is in me,' and 'I will not permit them to make her to turn.' That which is [written] under the boat which is in front shall read, 'Thou shalt not be motionless, my son;' and the words which are written in an opposite direction shall read, 'Thy support is like life,' and 'The word is as the word there,' and 'Thy son is with me,' and 'Life, strength, and health be to thy nostrils!' And that which is behind Shu, near his shoulder, shall read, 'They keep ward,' and that which is behind him, written close to his feet in an opposite direction, shall read, 'Maat,' and 'They come in,' and 'I protect daily.' And that which is under the shoulder of the divine figure which is under the left leg, and is behind it shall read, 'He who sealeth all things.' That which is over his head, under the thighs of the Cow, and that which is by her legs shall read, 'Guardian of his exit.' That which is behind the two figures which are by her two legs, that is to say, over their heads, shall read, 'The Aged One who is adored as he goeth forth,' and the Aged One to whom praise is given when he goeth in.' That which is over the head of the two figures, and is between the two thighs of the Cow, shall read, 'Listener,' 'Hearer,' 'Sceptre of the Upper Heaven,' and 'Star' (?).

CHAPTER III

Then the majesty of this god spake unto Thoth, [saying] 'Let a call go forth for me to the Majesty of the god Seb, saying, "Come, with the utmost speed, at once."' And when the Majesty of Seb had come, the Majesty of this god said unto him, 'Let war be made against thy worms (or, serpents) which are in thee; verily, they shall have fear of me as long as I have being; but thou knowest their magical powers. Do thou go to the place where my father Nu is, and say thou unto him, 'Keep ward over the worms (or, serpents) which are in the earth and water.' And moreover, thou shalt make a writing for each of the nests of thy serpents which are there, saying, 'Keep ye guard [lest ye] cause injury to anything.' They shall know that I am removing myself [from them], but indeed I shall shine upon them. Since, however, they indeed wish for a father, thou shalt be a father unto them in this land for ever. Moreover, let good heed be taken to the men who have my words of power, and to those whose mouths have knowledge of such things; verily my own words of power are there, verily it shall not happen that any shall participate with me in my protection, by reason of the majesty which hath come into being before me. I will decree them to thy son Osiris, and their children shall be watched over, the hearts of their princes shall be obedient (or, ready) by reason of the magical powers of those who act according to their desire in all the earth through their words of power which are in their bodies.'

CHAPTER IV

And the majesty of this god said, 'Call to me the god Thoth,' and one brought the god to him forthwith. And the Majesty of this god said unto Thoth, 'Let us depart to a distance from heaven, from my place, because I would make light and the god of light (Khu) in the Tuat and [in] the Land of Caves. Thou shalt write down [the things which are] in it, and thou shalt punish those who are in it, that is to say, the workers who have worked iniquity (or, rebellion). Through thee I will keep away from the servants whom this heart [of mine] loatheth. Thou shalt be in my place (ast) ASTI, and thou shalt therefore be called, O Thoth, the 'Asti of Ra.' Moreover, I give thee power to send (hab) forth . . .; thereupon shall come into being the Ibis (habi) bird of Thoth. I moreover give thee [power] to lift up thine hand before the two Companies of the gods who are greater than thou, and what thou doest shall be fairer than [the work of] the god Khen; therefore shall the divine bird tekni of Thoth come into being. Moreover, I give thee [Power] to embrace (anh) the two heavens with thy beauties, and with thy rays of light; therefore shall come into being the Moon-god (Aah) of Thoth. Moreover, I give thee [power] to drive back (anan) the Ha-nebu; therefore shall come into being the dog-headed Ape (anan) of Thoth, and he shall act as governor for me. Moreover, thou art now in my place in the sight of all those who see thee and who present offerings to thee, and every being shall ascribe praise unto thee, O thou who art God.'

CHAPTER V

Whosoever shall recite the words of this composition over himself shall anoint himself with olive oil and with thick unguent, and he shall have propitiatory offerings on both his hands of incense, and behind his two ears shall be pure natron, and sweet-smelling salve shall be on his lips. He shall be arrayed in a new double tunic, and his body shall be purified with the water of the Nile-flood, and he shall have upon his feet a pair of sandals made of white [leather], and a figure of the goddess Maat shall be drawn upon his tongue with green-coloured ochre. Whensoever Thoth shall wish to recite this composition on behalf of Ra, he must perform a sevenfold (?) purification for three days, and priests and [ordinary] men shall do likewise. Whosoever shall recite the above words shall perform the ceremonies which are to be performed when this book is being read. And he shall make his place of standing (?) in a circle (or, at an angle) . . . which is beyond [him], and his two eyes shall be fixed upon himself, all his members shall be [composed], and his steps shall not carry him away [from the place]. Whosoever among men shall recite [these] words shall be like Ra on the day of his birth; and his possessions shall not become fewer, and his house shall never fall into decay, but shall endure for a million eternities.

Then the Aged One himself (i.e., Ra) embraced (?) the god Nu, and spake unto the gods who came forth in the east of the sky, 'Ascribe ye praise to the god, the Aged One, from whom I have come into being. I am he who made the heavens, and I set in order [the earth, and created the gods, and] I was with them for an exceedingly long period; then was born the year and . . . but my soul is older than it (i.e., time). It is the Soul of Shu, it is the Soul of Khnemu (?), it is the Soul of Heh, it is the Soul of Kek and Kerh (i.e., Night and Darkness), it is the Soul of Nu and of Ra, it is the Soul of Osiris, the lord of Tettu, it is the Soul of the Sebak Crocodile-gods and of the Crocodiles, it is the Soul of every god [who dwelleth] in the divine Snakes, it is the Soul of Apep in Mount Bakhau (i.e., the Mount of Sunrise), and it is the Soul of Ra which pervadeth the whole world.'

Whosoever sayeth [these words] worketh his own protection by means of the words of power, 'I am the god Hekau (i.e., the divine Word of power), and [I am] pure in my mouth, and [in] my belly; [I am] Ra from whom the gods proceeded. I am Ra, the Light-god (Khu).' When thou sayest [this], stop forth in the evening and in the morning on thine own behalf if thou wouldst make to fall the enemies of Ra. I am his Soul, and I am Heka.

Hail, thou lord of eternity, thou creator of everlastingness, who bringest to nought the gods who came forth from Ra, thou lord of thy god, thou prince who didst make what made thee, who art beloved by the fathers of the gods, on whose head are the pure words of power, who didst create the woman (erpit) that standeth on the south side of thee, who didst create the goddess who hath her face on her breast, and the serpent which standeth on his tail, with her eye on his belly, and with his tail on the earth, to whom Thoth giveth praises, and upon whom the heavens rest, and to whom Shu stretcheth out his two hands, deliver thou me from those two great gods who sit in the east of the sky, who act as wardens of heaven and as wardens of earth, and who make firm the secret places, and who are called 'Aaiu-su,' and 'Per-f-er-maa-Nu.' Moreover [there shall be] a purifying on the . . . day of the month . . . even according to the performance of the ceremonies in the oldest time.

Whosoever shall recite this Chapter shall have life in Neter-kher (i.e., Underworld), and the fear of him shall be much greater than it was formerly [upon earth] . . . and they shall say, 'Thy names are 'Eternity' and 'Everlastingness.'' They are called, they are called, 'Au-peh-nef-n-aa-em-ta-uat-apu,' and 'Rekh-kua-[tut]-en-neter-pui-en en-hra-f-Her-shefu.' I am he who hath strengthened the boat with the company of the gods, and his Shenit, and his Gods, by means of words of power.

RA AND ISIS

Translated by E. A. Wallis Budge

The original text of this very interesting legend is written in the hieratic character on a papyrus preserved at Turin, and was published by Pleyte and Rossi in their Corpus of Turin Papyri. It has already been seen that the god Ra, when retiring from the government of this world, took steps through Thoth to supply mankind with words of power and spells with which to protect themselves against the bites of serpents and other noxious reptiles. When we read the following legend of Ra and Isis we understand why Ra, though king of the gods, was afraid of the reptiles which lived in the kingdom of Keb. At this time Isis lived in the form of a woman who possessed the knowledge of spells and incantations.

The Chapter of the divine (or, mighty) god, who created himself, who made the heavens and the earth, and the breath of life, and fire, and the gods, and men, and beasts, and cattle, and reptiles, and the fowl of the air, and the fish, who is the king of men and gods, [who existeth] in one Form, [to whom] periods of one hundred and twenty years are as single years, whose names by reason of their multitude are unknowable, for [even] the gods know them not. Behold, the goddess Isis lived in the form of a woman, who had the knowledge of words [of power]. Her heart turned away in disgust from the millions of men, and she chose for herself the millions of the gods, but esteemed more highly the millions of the spirits. Was it not possible to become even as was Ra in heaven and upon earth, and to make [herself] mistress of the earth, and a [mighty] goddess – thus she meditated in her heart – by the knowledge of the Name of the holy god? Behold, Ra entered [heaven] each day at the head of his mariners, establishing himself upon the double throne of the two horizons. Now the divine one had become old, he dribbled at the mouth, and he let his emissions go forth from him upon the earth, and his spittle fell upon the ground. This Isis kneaded in her hand, with [some] dust, and she fashioned it in the form of a sacred serpent, and made it to have the form of a dart, so that none might be able to escape alive from it, and she left it lying upon the road whereon the great god travelled, according to his desire, about the two lands. Then the holy god rose up in the tabernacle of the gods in the great double house (life, strength, health!) among those who were in his train, and [as] he journeyed on his way according to his daily wont, the holy serpent shot its fang into him, and the living fire was departing from the god's own body, and the reptile destroyed the dweller among the cedars. And the mighty god opened his mouth, and the cry of His Majesty (life, strength, health!) reached unto the heavens, and the company of the gods said, 'What is it?' and his gods said, 'What is the matter?' And the god found [no words] wherewith to answer concerning himself. His jaws shook, his lips trembled, and the poison took possession of all his flesh just as Hapi (i.e., the Nile) taketh possession of the land through which he floweth. Then the great god made firm his heart (i.e., took courage) and he cried out to those who were in his following: – 'Come ye unto me, O ye who have come into being from my members, ye gods who have proceeded from me, for I would make you to know what hath happened. I have been smitten by some deadly thing, of which my heart hath no knowledge, and which I have neither seen with my eyes nor made with my hand; and I have no knowledge at all who hath done this to me. I have never before felt any pain like unto it, and no pain can be worse than this [is]. I am a Prince, the son of a Prince, and the divine emanation which was produced from a god. I am a Great One, the son of a Great One, and my father hath determined for me my name. I have multitudes of names, and I have multitudes of forms, and my being existeth in every god. I have been invoked (or, proclaimed?) by Temu and Heru-Hekennu. My father and my mother uttered my name, and [they] hid it in my body at my birth so that none of those who would use against me words of power might succeed in making their enchantments have dominion over me. I had come forth from my tabernacle to look upon that which I had made, and was making my way through the two lands which I had made, when a blow was aimed at me, but I know not of what kind. Behold, is it fire? Behold, is it water?

My heart is full of burning fire, my limbs are shivering, and my members have darting pains in them. Let there be brought unto me my children the gods, who possess words of magic, whose mouths are cunning [in uttering them], and whose powers reach up to heaven.' Then his children came unto him, and every god was there with his cry of lamentation; and Isis came with her words of magic, and the place of her mouth [was filled with] the breath of life, for the words which she putteth together destroy diseases, and her words make to live those whose throats are choked (i.e., the dead). And she said, 'What is this, O divine father? What is it? Hath a serpent shot his venom into thee? Hath a thing which thou hast fashioned lifted up its head against thee? Verily it shall be overthrown by beneficent words of power, and I will make it to retreat in the sight of thy rays.' The holy god opened his mouth, [saying], I was going along the road and passing through the two lands of my country, for my heart wished to look upon what I had made, when I was bitten by a serpent which I did not see; behold, is it fire? Behold, is it water? I am colder than water, I am hotter than fire, all my members sweat, I myself quake, mine eye is unsteady. I cannot look at the heavens, and water forceth itself on my face as in the time of the Inundation.' And Isis said unto Ra, 'O my divine father, tell me thy name, for he who is able to pronounce his name liveth.' [And Ra said], 'I am the maker of the heavens and the earth, I have knit together the mountains, and I have created everything which existeth upon them. I am the maker of the Waters, and I have made Meht-ur to come into being; I have made the Bull of his Mother, and I have made the joys of love to exist. I am the maker of heaven, and I have made to be hidden the two gods of the horizon, and I have placed the souls of the gods within them. I am the Being who openeth his eyes and the light cometh; I am the Being who shutteth his eyes and there is darkness. I am the Being who giveth the command, and the waters of Hapi (the Nile) burst forth, I am the Being whose name the gods know not. I am the maker of the hours and the creator of the days. I am the opener (i.e., inaugurator) of the festivals, and the maker of the floods of water. I am the creator of the fire of life whereby the works of the houses are caused to come into being. I am Khepera in the morning, and Ra (at the time of his culmination (i.e., noon), and Temu in the evening.' Nevertheless the poison was not driven from its course, and the great god felt no better. Then Isis said unto Ra, 'Among the things which thou hast said unto me thy name hath not been mentioned. O declare thou it unto me, and the poison shall come forth; for the person who hath declared his name shall live.' Meanwhile the poison burned with blazing fire and the heat thereof was stronger than that of a blazing flame. Then the Majesty of Ra, said, 'I will allow myself to be searched through by Isis, and my name shall come forth from my body and go into hers.' Then the divine one hid himself from the gods, and the throne in the Boat of Millions of Years was empty. And it came to pass that when it was the time for the heart to come forth [from the god], she said unto her son Horus, 'The great god shall bind himself by an oath to give his two eyes.' Thus was the great god made to yield up his name, and Isis, the great lady of enchantments, said, 'Flow on, poison, and come forth from Ra; let the Eye of Horus come forth from the god and shine (?) outside his mouth. I have worked, and I make the poison to fall on the ground, for the venom hath been mastered. Verily the name hath been taken away from the great god. Let Ra live, and let the poison die; and if the poison live then Ra shall die. And similarly, a certain man, the son of a certain man, shall live and the poison shall die.' These were the words which spake Isis, the great lady, the mistress of the gods, and she had knowledge of Ra in his own name. The above words shall be said over an image of Temu and an image of Heru-Hekennu, and over an image of Isis and an image of Horus.

THE BIRTH OF HORUS

Translated by E. A. Wallis Budge

The greater part of the text consists of a hymn to Osiris, which was probably composed under the XVIIIth Dynasty, when an extraordinary development of the cult of that god took place, and when he was placed by Egyptian theologians at the head of all the gods. Though unseen in the temples, his presence filled all Egypt, and his body formed the very substance of the country. He was the God of all gods and the Governor of the Two Companies of the gods, he formed the soul and body of Ra, he was the beneficent Spirit of all spirits, he was himself the celestial food on which the Doubles in the Other World lived. He was the source of the Nile, the north wind sprang from him, his seats were the stars of heaven which never set, and the imperishable stars were his ministers. All heaven was his dominion, and the doors of the sky opened before him of their own accord when he appeared. He inherited the earth from his father Keb, and the sovereignty of heaven from his mother Nut.

Homage to thee, Osiris, Lord of eternity, King of the gods, whose names are manifold, whose transformations are sublime, whose form is hidden in the temples whose Ka is holy, the Governor of Tetut, the mighty one of possessions (?) in the shrine, the Lord of praises in the nome of Anetch, President of the tchefa food in Anu, Lord who art commemorated in [the town of] Maati, the mysterious (or, hidden) Soul, the Lord of Qerret, the sublime one in White Wall, the Soul of Ra [and] his very body, who hast thy dwelling in Henensu, the beneficent one, who art praised in Nart, who makest to rise up thy Soul, Lord of the Great House in the city of the Eight Gods, [who inspirest] great terror in Shas-hetep, Lord of eternity, Governor of Abtu (Abydos).

Thy seat (or, domain) reacheth far into Ta-tchesert, and thy name is firmly stablished in the mouth[s] of men. Thou art the two-fold substance of the Two Lands everywhere (?), and the divine food (tchef) of the Kau, the Governor of the Companies of the Gods, and the beneficent (or, perfect) Spirit-soul among Spirit-souls. The god Nu draweth his waters from thee, and thou bringest forth the north wind at eventide, and wind from thy nostrils to the satisfaction of thy heart. Thy heart flourisheth, and thou bringest forth the splendour of tchef food.

The height of heaven and the stars [thereof] are obedient unto thee, and thou makest to be opened the great gates [of the sky]. Thou art the lord to whom praises are sung in the southern heaven, thou art he to whom thanks are given in the northern heaven. The stars which never diminish are under the place of thy face, and thy seats are the stars which never rest. Offerings appear before thee by the command of Keb. The Companies of the Gods ascribe praise unto thee, the Star-gods of the Tuat smell the earth before thee, the domains [make] bowings [before thee], and the ends of the earth make supplication to thee [when] they see thee.

Those who are among the holy ones are in terror of him, and the Two Lands, all of them, make acclamations to him when they meet His Majesty. Thou art a shining Noble at the head of the nobles, permanent in [thy] high rank, stablished in [thy] sovereignty, the beneficent Power of the Company of the Gods. Well-pleasing [is thy] face, and thou art beloved by him that seeth thee. Thou settest the fear of thee in all lands, and because of their love for thee [men] hold thy name to be pre-eminent. Every man maketh offerings unto thee, and thou art the Lord who is commemorated in heaven and upon earth. Manifold are the cries of acclamation to thee in the Uak festival, and the Two Lands shout joyously to thee with one accord. Thou art the eldest, the first of thy brethren, the Prince of the Company of the Gods, and the stablisher of Truth throughout the Two Lands. Thou settest [thy] son upon the great throne of his father Keb. Thou art the beloved one of thy mother Nut, whose valour is most mighty [when] thou overthrowest the Seba Fiend. Thou hast slaughtered thy enemy, and hast put the fear of thee into thy Adversary.

Thou art the bringer in of the remotest boundaries, and art stable of heart, and thy two feet are lifted up (?); thou art the heir of Keb and of the sovereignty of the Two Lands, and he (i.e., Keb) hath seen thy splendid qualities, and hath commanded thee to guide the lands (i.e., the world) by thy hand so long as times [and seasons] endure.

Thou hast made this earth with thy hand, the waters thereof, the winds thereof, the trees and herbs thereof, the cattle thereof of every kind, the birds thereof of every kind, the fish thereof of every kind, the creeping things thereof, and the four-footed beasts thereof. The land of the desert belongeth by right to the son of Nut, and the Two Lands have contentment in making him to rise upon the throne of his father like Ra.

Thou rollest up into the horizon, thou settest the light above the darkness, thou illuminest [the Two Lands] with the light from thy two plumes, thou floodest the Two Lands like the Disk at the beginning of the dawn. Thy White Crown pierceth the height of heaven saluting the stars, thou art the guide of every god. Thou art perfect in command and word. Thou art the favoured one of the Great Company of the Gods, and thou art the beloved one of the Little Company of the Gods.

Thy sister [Isis] acted as a protectress to thee. She drove [thy] enemies away, she averted seasons [of calamity from thee], she recited the word (or, formula) with the magical power of her mouth, [being] skilled of tongue and never halting for a word, being perfect in command and word. Isis the magician avenged her brother. She went about seeking for him untiringly.

She flew round and round over this earth uttering wailing cries of grief, and she did not alight on the ground until she had found him. She made light [to come forth] from her feathers, she made air to come into being by means of her two wings, and she cried out the death cries for her brother. She made to rise up the helpless members of him whose heart was at rest, she drew from him his essence, and she made therefrom an heir. She suckled the child in solitariness and none knew where his place was, and he grew in strength. His hand is mighty (or, victorious) within the house of Keb, and the Company of the Gods rejoice greatly at the coming of Horus, the son of Osiris, whose heart is firmly stablished, the triumphant one, the son of Isis, the flesh and bone of Osiris. The Tchatcha of Truth, and the Company of the Gods, and Nebertcher himself, and the Lords of Truth, gather together to him, and assemble therein. Verily those who defeat iniquity rejoice in the House of Keb to bestow the divine rank and dignity upon him to whom it belongeth, and the sovereignty upon him whose it is by right.

HORUS AND THE WINGED DISK

Translated by E. A. Wallis Budge

The text of this legend is cut in hieroglyphics on the walls of the temple of Edfu in Upper Egypt, and certain portions of it are illustrated by large bas-reliefs. The legend, in the form in which it is here given, dates from the Ptolemaic Period, but the matter which it contains is far older, and it is probable that the facts recorded in it are fragments of actual history, which the Egyptians of the late period tried to piece together in chronological order. The great fact which he wished to describe is the conquest of Egypt by an early king, who, having subdued the peoples in the South, advanced northwards, and made all the people whom he conquered submit to his yoke. Now the King of Egypt was always called Horus, and the priests of Edfu wishing to magnify their local god, Horus of Behutet, or Horus of Edfu, attributed to him the conquests of this human, and probably predynastic, king. We must remember

that the legend assumes that Ra was still reigning on earth, though he was old and feeble, and had probably deputed his power to his successor, whom the legend regards as his son.

In the three hundred and sixty-third year of Ra-Heru-Khuti, who liveth for ever and forever, His Majesty was in Ta-Kens, and his soldiers were with him; [the enemy] did not conspire (auu) against their lord, and the land [is called] Uauatet unto this day. And Ra set out on an expedition in his boat, and his followers were with him, and he arrived at Uthes-Heru, [which lay to] the west of this nome, and to the east of the canal Pakhennu, which is called [. . . to this day]. And Heru-Behutet was in the boat of Ra, and he said unto his father Ra-Heru-Khuti (i.e., Ra-Harmachis), 'I see that the enemies are conspiring against their lord; let thy fiery serpent gain the mastery . . . over them.'

Then the Majesty of Ra-Harmachis said unto thy divine Ka, 'O Heru-Behutet, O son of Ra, thou exalted one, who didst proceed from me, overthrow thou the enemies who are before thee straightway.' And Heru-Behutet flew up into the horizon in the form of the great Winged Disk, for which reason he is called 'Great god, lord of heaven,' unto this day. And when he saw the enemies in the heights of heaven he set out to follow after them in the form of the great Winged Disk, and he attacked with such terrific force those who opposed him, that they could neither see with their eyes nor hear with their ears, and each of them slew his fellow. In a moment of time there was not a single creature left alive. Then Heru-Behutet, shining with very many colours, came in the form of the great Winged Disk to the Boat of Ra-Harmachis, and Thoth said unto Ra, 'O Lord of the gods, Behutet hath returned in the form of the great Winged Disk, shining [with many colours] . . . children;' for this reason he is called Heru-Behutet unto this day. And Thoth said, 'The city Teb shall be called the city of Heru-Behutet,' and thus is it called unto this day. And Ra embraced the . . . of Ra, and said unto Heru-Behutet, 'Thou didst put grapes into the water which cometh forth from it, and thy heart rejoiced thereat;' and for this reason the water (or, canal) of Heru-Behutet is called '[Grape-Water]' unto this day, and the . . . unto this day. And Heru-Behutet said, 'Advance, O Ra, and look thou upon thine enemies who are lying under thee on this land;' thereupon the Majesty of Ra set out on the way, and the goddess Asthertet ('Ashtoreth?) was with him, and he saw the enemies overthrown on the ground, each one of them being fettered. Then said Ra to Heru-Behutet, 'There is sweet life in this place,' and for this reason the abode of the palace of Heru-Behutet is called 'Sweet Life' unto this day. And Ra, said unto Thoth, '[Here was the slaughter] of mine enemies'; and the place is called Teb unto this day. And Thoth said unto Heru-Behutet, 'Thou art a great protector (makaa);' and the Boat of Heru-Behutet is called Makaa unto this day. Then said Ra unto the gods who were in his following, 'Behold now, let us sail in our boat upon the water, for our hearts are glad because our enemies have been overthrown on the earth;' and the water where the great god sailed is called P-Khen-Ur unto this day. And behold the enemies [of Ra] rushed into the water, and they took the forms of [crocodiles and] hippopotami, but nevertheless

Ra-Heru-Khuti sailed over the waters in his boat, and when the crocodiles and the hippopotami had come nigh unto him, they opened wide their jaws in order to destroy Ra-Heru-Khuti. And when Heru-Behutet arrived and his followers who were behind him in the forms of workers in metal, each having in his hands an iron spear and a chain, according to his name, they smote the crocodiles and the hippopotami; and there were brought in there straightway six hundred and fifty-one crocodiles, which had been slain before the city of Edfu. Then spake Ra-Harmachis unto Heru-Behutet, 'My Image shall be [here] in the land of the South, (which is a house of victory (or, strength)'; and the House of Heru-Behutet is called Nekht-Het unto this day.

Then the god Thoth spake, after he had looked upon the enemies lying upon the ground, saying, 'Let your hearts rejoice, O ye gods of heaven! Let your hearts rejoice, O ye gods who are in the earth! Horus, the Youthful One, cometh in peace, and he hath made manifest on his journey deeds of very great might, which he hath performed according to "the Book of Slaying the Hippopotamus". And from that day figures of Heru-Behutet in metal have existed.

Then Heru-Behutet took upon himself the form of the Winged Disk, and he placed himself upon the front of the Boat of Ea. And he placed by his side the goddess Nekhebet and the goddess Uatchet, in the form of two serpents, that they might make the enemies to quake in [all] their limbs when they were in the forms of crocodiles and hippopotami in every place wherein be came in the Land of the South and in the Land of the North. Then those enemies rose up to make their escape from before him, and their face was towards the Land of the South. And their hearts were stricken down through fear of him. And Heru-Behutet was at the back (or, side) of them in the Boat of Ra, and there were in his hands a metal lance and a metal chain; and the metal workers who were with their lord were equipped for fighting with lances and chains. And Heru-Behutet saw them to the south-east of the city of Uast (Thebes) some distance away. Then Ra said to Thoth, 'Those enemies shall be smitten with blows that kill;' and Thoth said to Ra, '[That place] is called the city Tchet-Met unto this day.' And Heru-Behutet made a great overthrow among them, and Ra said, 'Stand still, O Heru-Behutet,' and [that place] is called 'Het-Ra' to this day, and the god who dwelleth therein is Heru-Behutet-Ra-Amsu (or, Min). Then those enemies rose up to make their escape from before him, and the face of the god was towards the Land of the North, and their hearts were stricken through fear of him. And Heru-Behutet was at the back (or, side) of them in the Boat of Ra, and those who were following him had spears of metal and chains of metal in their hands; and the god himself was equipped for battle with the weapons of the metal workers which they had with them. And he passed a whole day before he saw them to the north-east of the nome of Tentyra (Dendera). Then Ra said unto Thoth, 'The enemies are resting . . . their lord.' And the Majesty of Ra-Harmachis said to Heru-Behutet, 'Thou art my exalted son who didst proceed from Nut. The courage of the enemies hath failed in a moment.' And Heru-Behutet made great slaughter among them. And Thoth said 'The Winged Disk shall be called . . . in the name of this Aat;' and is called Heru-Behutet . . . its mistress. His name is to the South in the name of this god, and the acacia and the sycamore shall be the trees of the sanctuary. Then the enemies turned aside to flee from before him, and their faces were [towards the North, and they went] to the swamps of Uatch-ur (i.e., the Mediterranean), and [their courage failed through fear of him]. And Heru-Behutet was at the back (or, side) of them in the Boat of Ra, and the metal spear was in his hands, and those who were in his following were equipped with the weapons for battle of the metal workers. And the god spent four days and four nights in the water in pursuit of them, but he did not see one of the enemies, who fled from before him in the water in the forms of crocodiles and hippopotami. At length he found them and saw them. And Ra said unto Horus of Heben, 'O Winged Disk, thou great god and lord of heaven, seize thou them . . .;' and he hurled his lance after them, and he slew them, and worked a great overthrow of them. And he brought one hundred and forty-two enemies to the forepart of the Boat [of Ra], and with them was a male hippopotamus which had been among those enemies. And he hacked them in pieces with his knife, and he gave their entrails to those who were in his following, and he gave their carcases to the gods and goddesses who were in the Boat of Ra on the river-bank of the city of Heben. Then Ra said unto Thoth, 'See what mighty things Heru-Behutet hath performed in his deeds against the enemies: verily he hath smitten them! And of the male hippopotamus he hath opened the mouth, and he hath speared it, and he hath mounted upon its back.' Then said Thoth to Ra, 'Horus shall be called 'Winged Disk, Great God, Smiter of the enemies in the town of Heben' from this day forward, and he shall be called "He who standeth on the back" and "prophet of this god", from this day forward.' These are the things which happened in the lands of the city of Heben, in a region which measured three hundred and forty-two measures on the south, and on the north, on the west, and on the east.

Then the enemies rose up before him by the Lake of the North, and their faces were set towards Uatch-ur which they desired to reach by sailing; but the god smote their hearts and they turned and fled in the water, and they directed their course to the water of the nome of Mertet-Ament, and they gathered themselves together in the water of Mertet in order to join themselves with the enemies [who serve] Set and who are in this region. And Heru-Behutet followed them, being equipped with all his weapons of war to fight against them. And Heru-Behutet made a journey in the Boat of Ra, together with the great god who was in his boat with those who were his followers, and he pursued them on the Lake of the North twice, and passed one day and one night sailing down the river in pursuit of them before he perceived and overtook them, for he knew not the place where they were. Then he arrived at the city of Per-Rehu. And the Majesty of Ra said unto Heru-Behutet, 'What hath happened to the enemies? They have gathered together themselves in the water to the west (?) of the nome of Mertet in order to unite themselves with the enemies [who serve] Set, and who are in this region, at the place where are our staff and sceptre.' And Thoth said unto Ra, 'Uast in the nome of Mertet is called Uaseb because of this unto this day, and the Lake which is in it is called Tempt.' Then Heru-Behutet spake in the presence of his father Ra, saying, 'I beseech thee to set thy boat against them, so that I may be able to perform against them that which Ra willeth;' and this was done. Then he made an attack upon them on the Lake which was at the west of this district, and he perceived them on the bank of the city . . . which belongeth to the Lake of Mertet. Then Heru-Behutet made an expedition against them, and his followers were with him, and they were provided with weapons of all kinds for battle, and he wrought a great overthrow among them, and he brought in three hundred and eighty-one enemies, and he slaughtered them in the forepart of the Boat of Ra, and he gave one of them to each of those who were in his train. Then Set rose up and came forth, and raged loudly with words of cursing and abuse because of the things which Heru-behutet had done in respect of the slaughter of the enemies. And Ra said unto Thoth, 'This fiend Nehaha-hra uttereth words at the top of his voice because of the things which Heru-Behutet hath done unto him;' and Thoth said unto Ra, 'Cries of this kind shall be called Nehaha-hra unto this day.' And Heru-Behutet did battle with the Enemy for a period of time, and he hurled his iron lance at him, and he threw him down on the ground in this region, which is called Pa-Rerehtu unto this day. Then Heru-Behutet came and brought the Enemy with him, and his spear was in his neck, and his chain was round his hands and arms, and the weapon of Horus had fallen on his mouth and had closed it; and he went with him before his father Ra, who said, 'O

Horus, thou Winged Disk, twice great (Urui-Tenten) is the deed of valour which thou hast done, and thou hast cleansed the district.' And Ra, said unto Thoth, 'The palace of Heru-Behutet shall be called, "Lord of the district which is cleansed" because of this;' and [thus is it called] unto this day. And the name of the priest thereof is called Ur-Tenten unto this day. And Ra said unto Thoth, 'Let the enemies and Set be given over to Isis and her son Horus, and let them work all their heart's desire upon them.' And she and her son Horus set themselves in position with their spears in him at the time when there was storm (or, disaster) in the district, and the Lake of the god was called She-En-Aha from that day to this. Then Horus the son of Isis cut off the head of the Enemy [Set], and the heads of his fiends in the presence of father Ra and of the great company of the gods, and he dragged him by his feet through his district with his spear driven through his head and back. And Ra said unto Thoth, 'Let the son of Osiris drag the being of disaster through his territory;' and Thoth said, 'It shall be called Ateh,' and this hath been the name of the region from that day to this. And Isis, the divine lady, spake before Ra, saying, 'Let the exalted Winged Disk become the amulet of my son Horus, who hath cut off the head of the Enemy and the heads of his fiends.'

Thus Heru-Behutet and Horus, the son of Isis, slaughtered that evil Enemy, and his fiends, and the inert foes, and came forth with them to the water on the west side of this district. And Heru-Behutet was in the form of a man of mighty strength, and he had the face of a hawk, and his head was crowned with the White Crown and the Red Crown, and with two plumes and two uraei, and he had the back of a hawk, and his spear and his chain were in his hands. And Horus, the son of Isis, transformed himself into a similar shape, even as Heru-Behutet had done before him. And they slew the enemies all together on the west of Per-Rehu, on the edge of the stream, and this god hath sailed over the water wherein the enemies had banded themselves together against him from that day to this. Now these things took place on the seventh day of the first month of the season Pert. And Thoth said, 'This region shall be called AAT-SHATET,' and this hath been the name of the region from that day unto this; and the Lake which is close by it hath been called Temt from that day to this, and the seventh day of the first month of the season Pert hath been called the Festival of Sailing from that day to this.

Then Set took upon himself the form of a hissing serpent, and he entered into the earth in this district without being seen. And Ra said, 'Set hath taken upon himself the form of a hissing serpent. Let Horus, the son of Isis, in the form of a hawk-headed staff, set himself over the place where he is, so that the serpent may never more appear.' And Thoth said, 'Let this district be called Hemhemet by name;' and thus hath it been called from that day to this. And Horus, the son of Isis, in the form of a hawk-headed staff, took up his abode there with his mother Isis; in this manner did these things happen.

This name means 'the place of the Roarer', Hemhemti, being a well-known name of the Evil One. Some texts seem to indicate that peals of thunder were caused by the fiend Set.

Then the Boat of Ra arrived at the town of Het-Aha; its forepart was made of palm wood, and the hind part was made of acacia wood; thus the palm tree and the acacia tree have been sacred trees from that day to this. Then Heru-Behutet embarked in the Boat of Ra, after he had made an end of fighting, and sailed; and Ra said unto Thoth, 'Let this Boat be called . . .;' and thus hath it been called from that day to this, and these things have been done in commemoration in this place from that day to this.

And Ra said unto Heru-Behutet, 'Behold the fighting of the Smait fiend and his two-fold strength, and the Smai fiend Set, are upon the water of the North, and they will sail down stream upon…' [And] Heru-Behutet said, 'Whatsoever thou commandest shall take place, O Ra, Lord of the gods. Grant thou, however, that this thy Boat may pursue them into every place whithersoever they shall go, and I will do to them whatsoever pleaseth Ra.' And everything was done according to what he had said. Then this Boat of Ra was brought by the winged Sun-disk upon the waters of the Lake of Meh, [and] Heru-Behutet took in his hands his weapons, his darts, and his harpoon, and all the chains [which he required] for the fight.

And Heru-Behutet looked and saw one [only] of these Sebau fiends there on the spot, and he was by himself. And he threw one metal dart, and brought (or, dragged) them along straightway, and he slaughtered them in the presence of Ra. And he made an end [of them, and there were no more of the fiends] of Set in this place at [that] moment.

'Sebiu' is a common name for the associates of Seti, and this fiend is himself called 'Seba', a word which means something like 'rebel'.

And Thoth said, 'This place shall be called Ast-Ab-Heru' because Heru-Behutet wrought his desire upon them (i.e., the enemy); and he passed six days and six nights coming into port on the waters thereof and did not see one of them. And he saw them fall down in the watery depths, and he made ready the place of Ast-ab-Heru there. It was situated on the bank of the water, and the face (i.e., direction) thereof was full-front towards the South. And all the rites and ceremonies of Heru-Behutet were performed on the first day of the first month of the season Akhet, and on the first day of the first month of the season Pert, and on the twenty-first and twenty-fourth days of the second month of the season Pert. These are the festivals in the town of Ast-ab, by the side of the South, in An-rut-f. And he came into port and went against them, keeping watch as for a king over the Great God in An-rut-f, in this place, in order to drive away the Enemy and his Smaiu fiends at his coming by night from the region of Mertet, to the west of this place.

And Heru-Behutet was in the form of a man who possessed great strength, with the face of a hawk; and he was crowned with the White Crown, and the Red Crown, and the two plumes, and the Urerit Crown, and there were two uraei upon his head. His hand grasped firmly his harpoon to slay the hippopotamus, which was [as hard] as the khenem stone in its mountain bed.

And Ra said unto Thoth, 'Indeed [Heru-]Behutet is like a Master-fighter in the slaughter of his enemies . . .'

And Thoth said unto Ra, 'He shall be called "Neb-Ahau"' (i.e., Master-fighter); and for this reason he hath been thus called by the priest of this god unto this day.

And Isis made incantations of every kind in order to drive away the fiend Ra from An-rut-f, and from the Great God in this place. And Thoth said [unto Ra], 'The priestess of this god shall be called by the name of "Nebt-Heka" for this reason.'

And Thoth said unto Ra, 'Beautiful, beautiful is this place wherein thou hast taken up thy seat, keeping watch, as for a king, over the Great God who is in An-rut-f in peace.'

And Thoth said, 'This Great House in this place shall therefore be called "Ast-Nefert" from this day. It is situated to the south-west of the city of Nart, and [covereth] a space of four schoinoi.' And Ra Heru-Behutet said unto Thoth, 'Hast thou not searched through this water for the enemy?' And Thoth said, 'The water of the God-house in this place shall be called by the name of "Heh" (i.e., sought out).' And Ra said, 'Thy ship, O Heru-Behutet, is great (?) upon Ant-mer (?) . . . And Thoth said, 'The name of [thy ship] shall be called "Ur", and this stream shall be called "Ant-mer (?)."' As concerning (or, now) the place Ab-Bat (?) is situated on the shore of the water. 'Ast-nefert' is the name of the Great house, 'Neb-Aha' [is the name of] the priest . . . is the name of the priestess, 'Heh' is the name of the lake . . . [is the name] of the water, 'Am-her-net' is the name of the holy (?) acacia tree, 'Neter het' is the name of the domain of the god, 'Uru' is the name of the sacred boat, the gods therein are Heru-Behutet, the smiter of the lands, Horus, the son of Isis [and]

Osiris . . . his blacksmiths are to him, and those who are in his following are to him in his territory, with his metal lance, with his [mace], with his dagger, and with all his chains (or, fetters) which are in the city of Heru-Behutet.

And Ra, said unto Thoth, 'My heart [is satisfied] with the works of these blacksmiths of Heru-Behutet who are in his bodyguard. They shall dwell in sanctuaries, and libations and purifications and offerings shall be made to their images, and [there shall be appointed for them] priests who shall minister by the month, and priests who shall minister by the hour, in all their God-houses whatsoever, as their reward because they have slain the enemies of the god.'

And Thoth said, 'The [Middle] Domains shall be called after the names of these blacksmiths from this day onwards, and the god who dwelleth among them, Heru-Behutet, shall be called the "Lord of Mesent" from this day onwards, and the domain shall be called "Mesent of the West" from this day onwards.'

As concerning Mesent of the West, the face (or, front) thereof shall be towards [the East], towards the place where Ra riseth, and this Mesent shall be called 'Mesent of the East' from this day onwards. As concerning the double town of Mesent, the work of these blacksmiths of the East, the face (or, front) thereof shall be towards the South, towards the city of Behutet, the hiding-place of Heru-Behutet. And there shall be performed therein all the rites and ceremonies of Heru-Behutet on the second day of the first month of the season of Akhet, and on the twenty-fourth day of the fourth month of the season of Akhet, and on the seventh day of the first month of the season Pert, and on the twenty-first day of the second month of the season Pert, from this day onwards. Their stream shall be called 'Asti', the name of their Great House shall be called 'Abet', the [priest (?)] shall be called 'Qen-aha', and their domain shall be called 'Kau-Mesent' from this day onwards.

And Ra said unto Heru-Behutet, 'These enemies have sailed up the river, to the country of Setet, to the end of the pillar-house of Hat, and they have sailed up the river to the east, to the country or Tchalt (or, Tchart), which is their region of swamps.' And Heru-Behutet said, 'Everything which thou hast commanded hath come to pass, Ra, Lord of the Gods; thou art the lord of commands.' And they untied the Boat of Ra, and they sailed up the river to the east. Then he looked upon those enemies whereof some of them had fallen into the sea (or, river), and the others had fallen headlong on the mountains.

And Heru-Behutet transformed himself into a lion which had the face of a man, and which was crowned with the triple crown. His paw was like unto a flint knife, and he went round and round by the side of them, and brought back one hundred and forty-two [of the enemy], and he rent them in pieces with his claws. He tore out their tongues, and their blood flowed on the ridges of the land in this place; and he made them the property of those who were in his following [whilst] he was upon the mountains.

And Thoth said, 'This domain shall be called "Khent-abt", and it shall [also] be called "Tchalt" (or, Tchart) from this day onwards. And the bringing of the tongues from the remote places of Tchalt (or, Tchart) [shall be commemorated] from this day onwards. And this god shall be called "Heru-Behutet, Lord of Mesent", from this day onwards.'

And Ra said unto Heru-Behutet, 'Let us sail to the south up the river, and let us smite the enemies [who are] in the forms of crocodiles and hippopotami in the face of Egypt.'

And Heru-Behutet said, 'Thy divine Ka, O Ra, Lord of the gods! Let us sail up the river against the remainder – one third – of the enemies who are in the water (or, river).' Then Thoth recited the Chapters of protecting the Boat [of Ra] and the boats of the blacksmiths, [which he used] for making tranquil the sea at the moment when a storm was raging on it.

And Ra said unto Thoth, 'Have we not journeyed throughout the whole land? Shall we not journey cover the whole sea in like manner?' And Thoth said, 'This water shall be called the "Sea of journeying", from this day onward.'

And they sailed about over the water during the night, and they did not see any of those enemies at all.

Then they made a journey forth and arrived in the country of Ta-Sti, at the town of Shas-hertet, and he perceived the most able of their enemies in the country of Uaua, and they were uttering treason against Horus their Lord.

And Heru-Behut changed his form into that of the Winged Disk, [and took his place] above the bow of the Boat of Ra. And he made the goddess Nekhebit and the goddess Uatchit to be with him in the form of serpents, so that they might make the Sebau fiends to quake in [all] their limbs (or, bodies). Their boldness (i.e., that of the fiends) subsided through the fear of him, they made no resistance whatsoever, and they died straightway.

Then the gods who were in the following of the Boat of Heru-khuti said, 'Great, great is that which he hath done among them by means of the two Serpent Goddesses, for he hath overthrown the enemy by means of their fear of him.'

And Ra-Heru-khuti said, 'The great one of the two Serpent Goddesses of Heru-Behutet shall be called "Ur-Uatchti" from this day onwards.'

And Heru-khuti travelled on in his boat, and landed at the city of Thes-Heru (Apollinopolis Magna). And Thoth said, 'The being of light who hath come forth from the horizon hath smitten the enemy in the form which he hath made, and he shall be called Being of light who hath come forth from the horizon from this day onwards.'

And Ra-Heru-khuti (Ra-Harmachis) said to Thoth, 'Thou shalt make this Winged Disk to be in every place wherein I seat myself (or, dwell), and in [all] the seats of the gods in the South, and in [all] the seats of the gods in the Land of the North . . . in the Country of Horus, that it may drive away the evil ones from their domains.'

Then Thoth made the image of the Winged Disk to be in every sanctuary and in every temple, where they now are, wherein are all the gods and all the goddesses from this day onwards. Now through the Winged Disk which is on the temple-buildings of all the gods and all the goddesses of the Land of the Lily, and the Land of the Papyrus, [these buildings] become shrines of Heru-Behutet.

As concerning Heru-Behutet, the great god, the lord of heaven, the president of the Ater of the South, he it is who is made to be on the right hand. This is Heru-Behutet on whom the goddess Nekhebit is placed in the form of a serpent (or, uraeus). As concerning Heru-Behutet, the great god, the lord of heaven, the lord of Mesent, the president of the Ater of the North, he it is who is made to be on the left hand. This Heru-Behutet on whom the goddess Uatchit is placed is in the form of a serpent.

As concerning Heru-Behutet, the great god, the lord of heaven, the lord of Mesent, the president of the two Aterti of the South and North, Ra-Heru-khuti set it (i.e., the Winged Disk) in his every place, to overthrow the enemies in every place wherein they are. And he shall be called President of the two Aterti of the South and North because of this from this day onwards.

THE DEATH AND RESURRECTION OF HORUS

Translated by E. A. Wallis Budge

The magical and religious texts of the Egyptians of all periods contain spells intended to be used against serpents, scorpions, and noxious reptiles of all kinds. All such creatures were regarded as incarnations of evil spirits, which attack the dead as well as the living, and therefore it was necessary for the well-being of the former that copies of spells against them should be written upon the walls of tombs, coffins, funerary amulets, etc. Towards the close of the XXVIth Dynasty, it became the custom to make house talismans in the form of small stone stelae. They are usually called 'Cippi of Horus'. The largest and most important of all these 'cippi' is that which is commonly known as the 'Metternich Stele'. It was dug up in 1828 in Alexandria and it was made between 378 BC and 360 BC. The first spell is an incantation directed against reptiles and noxious creatures in general. The next spell is directed to be said to the Cat, i.e., a symbol of the daughter of Ra, or Isis. In the next section, Ra-Harmakhis is called upon to come to his daughter, and Shu to his wife, and Isis to her sister, who has been poisoned. At this point on the Stele the spells are interrupted by a long narrative put into the mouth of Isis, which supplies us with some account of the troubles that she suffered, and describes the death of Horus through the sting of a scorpion. The Metternich Stele records a legend of Isis and Horus which is not found so fully described on any other monument.

INCANTATIONS AGAINST REPTILES AND NOXIOUS CREATURES IN GENERAL

Get thee back, Apep, thou enemy of Ra, thou winding serpent in the form of an intestine, without arms [and] without legs. Thy body cannot stand upright so that thou mayest have therein being, long is thy tail in front of thy den, thou enemy; retreat before Ra. Thy head shall be cut off, and the slaughter of thee shall be carried out. Thou shalt not lift up thy face, for his (i.e., Ra's) flame is in thy accursed soul. The odour which is in his chamber of slaughter is in thy members, and thy form shall be overthrown by the slaughtering knife of the great god. The spell of the Scorpion-goddess Serq driveth back thy might. Stand still, stand still, and retreat through her spell.

Be vomited, O poison, I adjure thee to come forth on the earth. Horus uttereth a spell over thee, Horus hacketh thee in pieces, he spitteth upon thee; thou shalt not rise up towards heaven, but shalt totter downwards, O feeble one, without strength, cowardly, unable to fight, blind, without eyes, and with thine head turned upside down. Lift not up thy face. Get thee back quickly, and find not the way. Lie down in despair, rejoice not, retreat speedily, and show not thy face because of the speech of Horus, who is perfect in words of power. The poison rejoiced, [but] the heart[s] of many were very sad thereat. Horus hath smitten it with his magical spells, and he who was in sorrow is [now] in joy. Stand still then, O thou who art in sorrow, [for] Horus hath been endowed with life. He coineth charged, appearing himself to overthrow the Sebiu fiends which bite. All men when they see Ra praise the son of Osiris. Get thee back, Worm, and draw out thy poison which is in all the members of him that is under the knife. Verily the might of the word of power of Horus is against thee. Vomit thou, O Enemy, get thee back, O poison.

THE CHAPTER OF CASTING A SPELL ON THE CAT

Recite [the following formula]: –

'Hail, Ra, come to thy daughter! A scorpion hath stung her on a lonely road. Her cry hath penetrated the heights of heaven, and is heard along the paths. The poison hath entered into her body, and circulateth through her flesh. She hath set her mouth against it; verily the poison is in her members.

'Come then with thy strength, with thy fierce attack, and with thy red powers, and force it to be hidden before thee. Behold, the poison hath entered into all the members of this Cat which is under my fingers. Be not afraid, be not afraid, my daughter, my splendour, [for] I have set myself near (or, behind) thee. I have overthrown the poison which is in all the limbs of this Cat. O thou Cat, thy head is the head of Ra, the Lord of the Two Lands, the smiter of the rebellious peoples. Thy fear is in all lands, O Lord of the living, Lord of eternity. O thou Cat, thy two eyes are the Eye of the Lord of the Khut uraeus, who illumineth the Two Lands with his Eye, and illumineth the face on the path of darkness. O thou Cat, thy nose is the nose of Thoth, the Twice Great, Lord of Khemenu (Hermopolis), the Chief of the Two Lands of Ra, who putteth breath into the nostrils of every person. O thou Cat, thine ears are the ears of Nebertcher, who hearkeneth unto the voice of all persons when they appeal to him, and weigheth words (i.e., judgeth) in all the earth. O thou Cat, thy mouth is the mouth of Tem, the Lord of life, the uniter (?) of creation, who hath caused the union (?) of creation; he shall deliver thee from every poison. O thou Cat, thy neck (nehebt) is the neck of Neheb-ka, President of the Great House, vivifier of men and women by means of the mouth of his two arms. O thou Cat, thy breast is the breast of Thoth, the Lord of Truth, who hath given to thee breath to refresh (?) thy throat, and hath given breath to that which is therein. O thou Cat, thy heart is the heart of the god Ptah, who healeth thy heart of the evil poison which is in all thy limbs. O thou Cat, thy hands are the hands of the Great Company of the gods and the Little Company of the gods, and they shall deliver thy hand from the poison from the mouth of every serpent. O thou Cat, thy belly is the belly of Osiris, Lord of Busiris, the poison shall not work any of its wishes in thy belly. O thou Cat, thy thighs are the thighs of the god Menthu, who shall make thy thighs to stand up, and shall bring the poison to the ground. O thou Cat, thy leg-bones are the leg-bones of Khensu, who travelleth over all the Two Lands by day and by night, and shall lead the poison to the ground. O thou Cat, thy legs (or, feet) are the legs of Amen the Great, Horus, Lord of Thebes, who shall stablish thy feet on the earth, and shall overthrow the poison. O thou Cat, thy haunches are the haunches of Horus, the avenger (or, advocate) of his father Osiris, and they shall place Set in the evil which he hath wrought. O thou Cat, thy soles are the soles of Ra, who shall make the poison to return to the earth. O thou Cat, thy bowels are the bowels of the Cow-goddess Meh-urt, who shall overthrow and cut in pieces the poison which is in thy belly and in all the members in thee, and in [all] the members of the gods in heaven, and in [all] the members of the gods on earth, and shall overthrow every poison in thee. There is no member in thee without the goddess who shall overthrow and cut in pieces the poison of every male serpent, and every female serpent, and every scorpion, and every reptile, which may be in any member of this Cat which is under the knife. Verily Isis weaveth and Nephthys spinneth against the poison. This woven garment strengtheneth this [being, i.e., Horus], who is perfect in words of power, through the speech of Ra-Heru-khuti, the great god, President of the South and North: "O evil poison which is in any member of this Cat which is under the knife, come, issue forth upon the earth.'"

ANOTHER CHAPTER

Say the [following] words: –

'O Ra-[Khuti], come to thy daughter. O Shu, come to thy wife. O Isis, come to thy sister, and deliver her from the evil poison which is in all her members. Hail, O ye gods, come ye and overthrow ye the evil poison which is in all the members of the Cat which is under the knife.

'Hail, O aged one, who renewest thy youth in thy season, thou old man who makest thyself to be a boy, grant thou that Thoth may come to me at [the sound of] my voice, and behold, let him turn back from me Netater. Osiris is on the water, the Eye of Horus is with him. A great Beetle spreadeth himself over him, great by reason of his grasp, produced by the gods from a child. He who is over the water appeareth in a healthy form. If he who is over the water shall be approached (or, attacked), the Eye of Horus, which weepeth, shall be approached.

'Get ye back, O ye who dwell in the water, crocodiles, fish, that Enemy, male dead person and female dead person, male fiend and female fiend, of every kind whatsoever, lift not up your faces, O ye who dwell in the waters, ye crocodiles and fish. When Osiris journeyeth over you, permit ye him to go to Busiris. Let your nostrils [be closed], your throats stopped up.

'Get ye back, Seba fiends! Lift ye not up your faces against him that is on the water . . . Osiris-Ra, riseth up in his Boat to look at the gods of Kher-ahat, and the Lords of the Tuat stand up to slay thee when [thou] comest, O Neha-her, against Osiris. [When] he is on the water the Eye of Horus is over him to turn your faces upside down and to set you on your backs.

'Hail, ye who dwell in the water, crocodiles and fish, Ra shutteth up your mouths, Sekhet stoppeth up your throats, Thoth cutteth out your tongues, and {cont} Heka blindeth your eyes. These are the four great gods who protect Osiris by their magical power, and they effect the protection of him that is on the water, of men and women of every kind, and of beasts and animals of every kind which are on the water by day. Protected are those who dwell in the waters, protected is the sky wherein is Ra, protected is the great god who is in the sarcophagus, protected is he who is on the water.

'A voice [which] crieth loudly is in the House of Net (Neith), a loud voice is in the Great House, a great outcry from the mouth of the Cat. The gods and the goddesses say, "What is it? What is it?" [It] concerneth the Abtu Fish which is born. Make to retreat from me thy footsteps, O Sebau fiend. I am Khnemu, the Lord of Her-urt. Guard thyself again from the attack which is repeated, besides this which thou hast done in the presence of the Great Company of the gods. Get thee back, retreat thou from me. I am the god. Oh, Oh, O [Ra], hast thou not heard the voice which cried out loudly until the evening on the bank of Netit, the voice of all the gods and goddesses which cried out loudly, the outcry concerning the wickedness which thou hast done, O wicked Sebau fiend? Verily the lord Ra thundered and growled thereat, and he ordered thy slaughter to be carried out. Get thee back, Seba fiend! Hail! Hail!'

THE NARRATIVE OF ISIS

I am Isis, [and] I have come forth from the dwelling (or, prison) wherein my brother Set placed me. Behold the god Thoth, the great god, the Chief of Maat [both] in heaven and on the earth, said unto me, 'Come now, O Isis, thou goddess, moreover it is a good thing to hearken, [for there is] life to one who shall be guided [by the advice] of another. Hide thou thyself with [thy] son the child, and there shall come unto him these things. His members shall grow, and two-fold strength of every kind shall spring up [in him]. [And he] shall be made to take his seat upon the throne of his father, [whom] he shall avenge, [and he shall take possession of] the exalted position of Heq of the Two Lands.'

I came forth [from the dwelling] at the time of evening, and there came forth the Seven Scorpions which were to accompany me and to strike (?) for me with [their] stings. Two scorpions, Tefen and Befen, were behind me, two scorpions, Mestet and Mestetef, were by my side, and three scorpions, Petet, Thetet, and Maatet (or, Martet), were preparing the road for me. I charged them very strictly (or, in a loud voice), and my words penetrated into their ears: 'Have no knowledge of [any], make no cry to the Tesheru beings, and pay no attention to the "son of a man" (i.e., anyone) who belongeth to a man of no account,' [and I said,] 'Let your faces be turned towards the ground [that ye may show me] the way.' So the guardian of the company brought me to the boundaries of the city of Pa-Sui, the city of the goddesses of the Divine Sandals, [which was situated] in front of the Papyrus Swamps.

When I had arrived at the place where the people lived I came to the houses wherein dwelt the wives [and] husbands. And a certain woman of quality spied me as I was journeying along the road, and she shut her doors on me. Now she was sick at heart by reason of those [scorpions] which were with me. Then [the Seven Scorpions] took counsel concerning her, and they all at one time shot out their venom on the tail of the scorpion Tefen; as for me, the woman Taha opened her door, and I entered into the house of the miserable lady.

Then the scorpion Tefen entered in under the leaves of the door and smote (i.e., stung) the son of Usert, and a fire broke out in the house of Usert, and there was no water there to extinguish it; [but] the sky rained upon the house of Usert, though it was not the season for rain.

Behold, the heart of her who had not opened her door to me was grievously sad, for she knew not whether he (i.e., her son) would live [or not], and although she went round about through her town uttering cries [for help], there was none who came at [the sound of] her voice. Now mine own heart was grievously sad for the sake of the child, and [I wished] to make to live [again] him that was free from fault. [Thereupon] I cried out to the noble lady, 'Come to me. Come to me. Verily my mouth (?) possesseth life. I am a daughter [well] known in her town, [and I] can destroy the demon of death by the spell (or, utterance) which my father taught me to know. I am his daughter, the beloved [offspring] of his body.'

Then Isis placed her two hands on the child in order to make to live him whose throat was stopped, [and she said], 'O poison of the scorpion Tefent, come forth and appear on the ground! Thou shalt neither enter nor penetrate [further into the body of the child]. O poison of the scorpion Befent, come forth and appear on the ground! I am Isis, the goddess, the lady (or, mistress) of words of power, and I am the maker of words of power (i.e., spells), and I know how to utter words with magical effect. Hearken ye unto me, O every reptile which possesseth the power to bite (i.e., to sting), and fall headlong to the ground! O poison of the scorpion Mestet, make no advance [into his body]. O poison of the scorpion Mestetef, rise not up [in his body]. O poison of the scorpions Petet and Thetet, penetrate not [into his body]. [O poison of] the scorpion Maatet (or, Martet), fall down on the ground.'

[Here follows the] 'Chapter of the stinging [of scorpions].'

And Isis, the goddess, the great mistress of spells (or, words of power), she who is at the head of the gods, unto whom the god Keb gave his own magical spells for the driving away of poison at noon-day (?), and for making poison to go back, and retreat, and withdraw, and go backward, spake, saying, 'Ascend not into heaven, through the command of the beloved one of Ra, the egg of the Smen goose which cometh forth from the sycamore. Verily my words are made to command the uttermost limit of the night. I speak unto you, [O scorpions] I am alone and in sorrow because our names will suffer disgrace throughout the nomes. Do not make love, do not cry out to the Tesheru fiends, and cast no glances upon the noble ladies in their houses. Turn your faces towards the earth and [find out] the road, so that we may arrive at the hidden places in the town of Khebt. Oh the child shall live and the poison die! Ra liveth and the poison dieth! Verily Horus shall be in good case (or, healthy) for his mother Isis. Verily he who is stricken shall be in good case likewise.'

And the fire [which was in the house of Usert] was extinguished, and heaven was satisfied with the utterance of Isis, the goddess.

Then the lady Usert came, and she brought unto me her possessions, and she filled the house of the woman Tah (?), for the Ka of Tah (?) because [she] had opened to me her door. Now the lady Usert suffered pain and anguish the whole night, and her mouth tasted (i.e., felt) the sting [which] her son [had suffered]. And she brought her possessions as the penalty for not having opened the door to me. Oh the child shall live and the poison die! Verily Horus shall be in good case for his mother Isis. Verily everyone who is stricken shall be in good case likewise.

Lo, a bread-cake [made] of barley meal shall drive out (or, destroy) the poison, and natron shall make it to withdraw, and the fire [made] of hetchet-plant shall drive out (or, destroy) fever-heat from the limbs.

'O Isis, O Isis, come thou to thy Horus, O thou woman of the wise mouth! Come to thy son' – thus cried the gods who dwelt in her quarter of the town – 'for he is as one whom a scorpion hath stung, and like one whom the scorpion Uhat, which the animal Antesh drove away, hath wounded.'

[Then] Isis ran out like one who had a knife [stuck] in her body, and she opened her arms wide, [saying] 'Behold me, behold me, my son Horus, have no fear, have no fear, O son my glory! No evil thing of any kind whatsoever shall happen unto thee, [for] there is in thee the essence (or, fluid) which made the things which exist. Thou art the son from the country of Mesqet, [thou hast] come forth from the celestial waters Nu, and thou shalt not die by the heat of the poison. Thou wast the Great Bennu, who art born (or, produced) or; the top of the balsam-trees which are in the House of the Aged One in Anu (Heliopolis). Thou art the brother of the Abtu Fish, who orderest what is to be, and art the nursling of the Cat who dwelleth in the House of Neith. The goddess Reret, the goddess Hat, and the god Bes protect thy members. Thy head shall not fall to the Tchat fiend that attacketh thee. Thy members shall not receive the fire of that which is thy poison. Thou shalt not go backwards on the land, and thou shalt not be brought low on the water. No reptile which biteth (or, stingeth) shall gain the mastery over thee, and no lion shall subdue thee or have dominion over thee. Thou art the son of the sublime god who proceeded from Keb. Thou art Horus, and the poison shall not gain the mastery over thy members. Thou art the son of the sublime god who proceeded from Keb, and thus likewise shall it be with those who are under the knife. And the four august goddesses shall protect thy members.'

[Here the narrative is interrupted by the following texts:]

[I am] he who rolleth up into the sky, and who goeth down (i.e., setteth) in the Tuat, whose form is in the House of height, through whom when he openeth his Eye the light cometh into being, and when he closeth his Eye it becometh night. [I am] the Water-god Het when he giveth commands, whose name is unknown to the gods. I illumine the Two Lands, night betaketh itself to flight, and I shine by day and by night. I am the Bull of Bakha, and the Lion of Manu. I am he who traverseth the heavens by day and by night without being repulsed. I have come by reason of the voice (or, cry) of the son of Isis. Verily the blind serpent Na hath bitten the Bull. O thou poison which floweth through every member of him that is under the knife, come forth, I charge thee, upon the ground. Behold, he that is under the knife shall not be bitten. Thou art Menu, the Lord of Coptos, the child of the White Shat which is in Anu (Heliopolis), which was bitten [by a reptile]. O Menu, Lord of Coptos, give thou air unto him that is under the knife; and air shall be given to thee. Hail, divine father and minister of the god Nebun, [called] Mer-Tem, son of the divine father and minister of the god Nebun, scribe of the Water-god Het, [called] Ankh-Semptek (sic), son of the lady of the house Tent-Het-nub! He restored this inscription after he had found it in a ruined state in the Temple of Osiris-Mnevis, because he wished to make to live her name . . . and to give air unto him that is under [the knife], and to give life unto the ancestors of all the gods. And his Lord Osiris-

Mnevis shall make long his life with happiness of heart, [and shall give him] a beautiful burial after [attaining to] an old age, because of what he hath done for the Temple of Osiris-Mnevis.

Horus was bitten (i.e., stung) in Sekhet-An, to the north of Hetep-hemt, whilst his mother Isis was in the celestial houses making a libation for her brother Osiris. And Horus sent forth his cry into the horizon, and it was heard by those who were in . . . Thereupon the keepers of the doors who were in the [temple of] the holy Acacia Tree started up at the voice of Horus. And one sent forth a cry of lamentation, and Heaven gave the order that Horus was to be healed. And [the gods] took counsel [together] concerning the life [of Horus, saying,] 'O goddess Pai(?), O god Asten, who dwellest in Aat-Khus(?) . . . thy . . . enter in . . . lord of sleep . . . the child Horus. Oh, Oh, bring thou the things which are thine to cut off the poison which is in every member of Horus, the son of Isis, and which is in every member of him that is under the knife likewise.'

A HYMN OF PRAISE TO HORUS TO GLORIFY HIM, WHICH IS TO BE SAID OVER THE WATERS AND OVER THE LAND.

Thoth speaketh and this god reciteth [the following]: –
    'Homage to thee, god, son of a god. Homage to thee, heir, son of an heir. Homage to thee, bull, son of a bull, who wast brought

forth by a holy goddess. Homage to thee, Horus, who comest forth from Osiris, and wast brought forth by the goddess Isis. I recite thy words of power, I speak with thy magical utterance. I pronounce a spell in thine own words, which thy heart hath created, and all the spells and incantations which have come forth from thy mouth, which thy father Keb commanded thee [to recite], and thy mother Nut gave to thee, and the majesty of the Governor of Sekhem taught thee to make use of for thy protection, in order to double (or, repeat) thy protective formulae, to shut the mouth of every reptile which is in heaven, and on the earth, and in the waters, to make men and women to live, to make the gods to be at peace [with thee], and to make Ra to employ his magical spells through thy chants of praise. Come to me this day, quickly, quickly, as thou workest the paddle of the Boat of the god. Drive thou away from me every lion on the plain, and every crocodile in the waters, and all mouths which bite (or, sting) in their holes. Make thou them before me like the stone of the mountain, like a broken pot lying about in a quarter of the town. Dig thou out from me the poison which riseth and is in every member of him that is under the knife. Keep thou watch over him . . . by means of thy words. Verily let thy name be invoked this day. Let thy power (qefau) come into being in him. Exalt thou thy magical powers. Make me to live and him whose throat is closed up. Then shall mankind give thee praise, and the righteous (?) shall give thanks unto thy forms. And all the gods likewise shall invoke thee, and in truth thy name shall be invoked this day. I am Horus [of] Shet[enu] (?).

'O thou who art in the cavern, O thou who art in the cavern. O thou who art at the mouth of the cavern. O thou who art on the way, O thou who art on the way. O thou who art at the mouth of the way. He is Urmer (Mnevis) who approacheth every man and every beast. He is like the god Sep who is in Anu (Heliopolis). He is the Scorpion-[god] who is in the Great House (Het-ur). Bite him not, for he is Ra. Sting him not, for he is Thoth. Shoot ye not your poison over him, for he is Nefer-Tem. O every male serpent, O every female serpent, O every antesh (scorpion?) which bite with your mouths, and sting with your tails, bite ye him not with your mouths, and sting ye him not with your tails. Get ye afar off from him, make ye not your fire to be against him, for he is the son of Osiris. Vomit ye. [Say] four times: —

'I am Thoth, I have come from heaven to make protection of Horus, and to drive away the poison of the scorpion which is in every member of Horus. Thy head is to thee, Horus; it shall be stable under the Urert Crown. Thine eye is to thee, Horus, [for] thou art Horus, the son of Keb, the Lord of the Two Eyes, in the midst of the Company [of the gods]. Thy nose is to thee, Horus, [for] thou art Horus the Elder, the son of Ra, and thou shalt not inhale the fiery wind. Thine arm is to thee, Horus, great is thy strength to slaughter the enemies of thy father. Thy two thighs are to thee, Horus. Receive thou the rank and dignity of thy father Osiris. Ptah hath balanced for thee thy mouth on the day of thy birth. Thy heart (or, breast) is to thee, Horus, and the Disk maketh thy protection. Thine eye is to thee, Horus; thy right eye is like Shu, and thy left eye like Tefnut, who are the children of Ra. Thy belly is to thee, Horus, and the Children are the gods who are therein, and they shall not receive the essence (or, fluid) of the scorpion. Thy strength is to thee, Horus, and the strength of Set shall not exist against thee. Thy phallus is to thee, Horus, and thou art Kamutef, the protector of his father, who maketh an answer for his children in the course of every day. Thy thighs are to thee, Horus, and thy strength shall slaughter the enemies of thy father. Thy calves are to thee, Horus; the god Khnemu hath builded [them], and the goddess Isis hath covered them with flesh. The soles of thy feet are to thee, Horus, and the nations who fight with the bow (Peti) fall under thy feet. Thou rulest the South, North, West, and East, and thou seest like Ra. [Say] four times. And likewise him that is under the knife.'

Beautiful god, Senetchem-ab-Ra-setep-[en]-Amen, son of Ra, Nekht-Heru-Hebit, thou art protected, and the gods and goddesses are protected, and conversely. Beautiful god, Senetchem-ab-Ra-setep-[en]-Ra, son of Ra, Nekht-Heru-Hebit, thou art protected, and Heru-Shet[enu], the great god, is protected, and conversely.

[Another chapter like unto it:]

'Fear not, fear not, O Bast, the strong of heart, at the head of the holy field, the mighty one among all the gods, nothing shall gain the mastery over thee. Come thou outside, following my speech (or, mouth), O evil poison which is in all the members of the lion (or, cat) which is under the knife.'

[The narrative of the stinging of Horus by a scorpion is continued thus]:

'I am Isis, who conceived a child by her husband, and she became heavy with Horus, the divine [child]. I gave birth to Horus, the son of Osiris, in a nest of papyrus plants. I rejoiced exceedingly over this, because I saw [in him one] who would make answer for his father. I hid him, and I concealed him through fear of that [fiend (?)]. I went away to the city of Am, [where] the people gave thanks [for me] through [their] fear of my making trouble [for them]. I passed the day in seeking to provide food for the child, [and] on returning to take Horus into my arms I found him, Horus, the beautiful one of gold, the boy, the child, without [life]. He had bedewed the ground with the water of his eye, and with foam from his lips. His body was motionless, his heart was powerless to move, and the sinews (or, muscles) of his members were [helpless]. I sent forth a cry, [saying]:

"'I, even I, lack a son to make answer [for me]. [My] two breasts are full to overflowing, [but] my body is empty. [My] mouth wished for that which concerned him. A cistern of water and a stream of the inundation was I. The child was the desire of my heart, and I longed to protect him (?). I carried him in my womb, I gave birth to him, I endured the agony of the birth pangs, I was all alone, and the great ones were afraid of disaster and to come out at the sound of my voice. My father is in the Tuat, my mother is in Aqert, and my elder brother is in the sarcophagus. Think of the enemy and of how prolonged was the wrath of his heart against me, [when] I, the great lady, was in his house."

'I cried then, [saying,] "Who among the people will indeed let their hearts come round to me?" I cried then to those who dwelt in the papyrus swamps (or, Ateh), and they inclined to me straightway. And the people came forth to me from their houses, and they thronged about me at [the sound of] my voice, and they loudly bewailed with me the greatness of my affliction. There was no man there who set restraint (?) on his mouth, every person among them lamented with great lamentation. There was none there who knew how to make [my child] to live.

'And there came forth unto me a woman who was [well] known in her city, a lady who was mistress of her [own] estate. She came forth to me. Her mouth possessed life, and her heart was filled with the matter which was therein, [and she said,] "Fear not, fear not, O son Horus! Be not cast down, be not cast down, O mother of the god. The child of the Olive-tree is by the mountain of his brother, the bush is hidden, and no enemy shall enter therein. The word of power of Tem, the Father of the gods, who is in heaven, maketh to live. Set shall not enter into this region, he shall not go round about it. The marsh of Horus of the Olive-tree is by the mountain of his brother; those who are in his following shall not at any time . . . it. This shall happen to him: Horus shall live for his mother, and shall salute (?) [her] with his mouth. A scorpion hath smitten (i.e., stung) him, and the reptile Aun-ab hath wounded him.'"

Then Isis placed her nose in his mouth so that she might know whether he who was in his coffin breathed, and she examined the wound of the heir of the god, and she found that there was poison in it. She threw her arms round him, and then quickly she leaped about with him like fish when they are laid upon the hot coals, [saying]:

'Horus is bitten, O Ra. Thy son is bitten, [O Osiris]. Horus is bitten, the flesh and blood of the Heir, the Lord of the diadems (?) of the kingdoms of Shu. Horus is bitten, the Boy of the marsh city of Ateh, the Child in the House of the Prince. The beautiful Child of gold is bitten, the Babe hath suffered pain and is not. Horus is bitten, he the son of Un-Nefer, who was born of Auh-mu (?). Horus is bitten, he in whom there was nothing abominable, the son, the youth among the gods. Horus is bitten, he for whose wants I prepared in abundance, for I saw that he would make answer for his father. Horus is bitten, he for whom [I] had care [when he was] in the hidden woman [and for whom I was afraid when he was] in the womb of his mother. Horus is bitten, he whom I guarded to look upon. I have wished for the life of his heart. Calamity hath befallen the child on the water, and the child hath perished.'

Then came Nephthys shedding tears and uttering cries of lamentation, and going round about through the papyrus swamps. And Serq [came also and they said]: 'Behold, behold, what hath happened to Horus, son of Isis, and who [hath done it]? Pray then to heaven, and let the mariners of Ra cease their labours for a space, for the Boat of Ra cannot travel onwards [whilst] son Horus [lieth dead] on his place.'

And Isis sent forth her voice into heaven, and made supplication to the Boat of Millions of Years, and the Disk stopped in its journeying, and moved not from the place whereon it rested. Then came forth Thoth, who is equipped with his spells (or, words of power), and possesseth the great word of command of maa-kheru, [and said:] 'What [aileth thee], what [aileth thee], O Isis, thou goddess who hast magical spells, whose mouth hath understanding? Assuredly no evil thing hath befallen [thy] son Horus, [for] the Boat of Ra hath him under its protection. I have come this day in the Divine Boat of the Disk from the place where it was yesterday – now darkness came and the light was destroyed – in order to heal Horus for his mother Isis and every person who is under the knife likewise.'

And Isis, the goddess, said: 'O Thoth, great things [are in] thy heart, [but] delay belongeth to thy plan. Hast thou come equipped with thy spells and incantations, and having the great formula of maa-kheru, and one [spell] after the other, the numbers whereof are not known? Verily Horus is in the cradle (?) of the poison. Evil, evil is his case, death, [and] misery to the fullest [extent]. The cry of his mouth is towards his mother (?). I cannot [bear] to see these things in his train. My heart [hath not] rested because of them since the beginning (?) [when] I made haste to make answer [for] Horus-Ra (?), placing [myself] on the earth, [and] since the day [when] I was taken possession of by him. I desired Neheb-ka . . . '

[And Thoth said:] 'Fear not, fear not, O goddess Isis, fear not, fear not, O Nephthys, and let not anxiety [be to you]. I have come from heaven having life to heal (?) the child for his mother, Horus is . . . Let thy heart be firm; he shall not sink under the flame. Horus is protected as the Dweller in his Disk, who lighteth up the Two Lands by the splendour of his two Eyes; and he who is under the knife is likewise protected. Horus is protected as the First-born son in heaven, who is ordained to be the guide of the things which exist and of the things which are not yet created; and he who under the knife is protected likewise. Horus is protected as that great Dwarf (nemu) who goeth round about the Two Lands in the darkness; and he who is under the knife is protected likewise. Horus is protected as the Lord (?) in the night, who revolveth at the head of the Land of the Sunset (Manu); and he who is under the knife is protected likewise. Horus is protected as the Mighty Ram who is hidden, and who goeth round about in front of his Eyes; and he who is under the knife is protected likewise. Horus is protected as the Great Hawk which flieth through heaven, earth, and the Other World (Tuat); and he who is under the knife is protected likewise. Horus is protected as the Holy Beetle, the mighty (?) wings of which are at the head of the sky; and he who is under the knife is protected likewise. Horus is protected as the Hidden Body, and as he whose mummy is in his sarcophagus; and he who is under the knife is protected likewise. Horus is protected [as the Dweller] in the Other World [and in the] Two Lands, who goeth round about "Those who are over Hidden Things"; and he who is under the knife is protected likewise. Horus is protected as the Divine Bennu who alighteth in front of his two Eyes; and he who is under the knife is protected likewise. Horus is protected in his own body, and the spells which his mother Isis hath woven protect him. Horus is protected by the names of his father [Osiris] in his forms in the nomes; and he who is under the knife is protected likewise. Horus is protected by the weeping of his mother, and by the cries of grief of his brethren; and he who is under the knife is protected likewise. Horus is protected by his own name and heart, and the gods go round about him to make his funeral bed; and he who is under the knife is protected likewise.'

[And Thoth said:]

'Wake up, Horus! Thy protection is established. Make thou happy the heart of thy mother Isis. The words of Horus shall bind up hearts, he shall cause to be at peace him who is in affliction. Let your hearts be happy, O ye who dwell in the heavens (Nut). Horus, he who hath avenged (or, protected) his father shall cause the poison to retreat. Verily that which is in the mouth of Ra shall go round about (i.e., circulate), and the tongue of the Great God shall repulse [opposition]. The Boat [of Ra] standeth still, and travelleth not onwards. The Disk is in the [same] place where it was yesterday to heal Horus for his mother Isis, and to heal him that is under the knife of his mother likewise. Come to the earth, draw nigh, O Boat of Ra, make the boat to travel, O mariners of heaven, transport provisions (?) of . . . Sekhem to heal Horus for his mother Isis, and to heal him that is under the knife of his mother likewise. Hasten away, O pain which is in the region round about, and let it (i.e., the Boat) descend upon the place where it was yesterday to heal Horus for his mother Isis, and to heal him that is under the knife of his mother likewise. Get thee round and round, O bald (?) fiend, without horns at the seasons (?), not seeing the forms through the shadow of the two Eyes, to heal Horus for his mother Isis, and to heal him that is under the knife likewise. Be filled, O two halves of heaven, be empty,

O papyrus roll, return, O life, into the living to heal Horus for his mother Isis, and to heal him that is under the knife likewise. Come thou to earth, O poison. Let hearts be glad, and let radiance (or, light) go round about.

'I am Thoth, the first-born son, the son of Ra, and Tem and the Company of the gods have commanded me to heal Horus for his mother Isis, and to heal him that is under the knife likewise. O Horus, O Horus, thy Ka protecteth thee, and thy Image worketh protection for thee. The poison is as the daughter of its [own] flame; [it is] destroyed [because] it smote the strong son. Your temples are in good condition for you, [for] Horus liveth for his mother, and he who is under the knife likewise.'

And the goddess Isis said:

'Set thou his face towards those who dwell in the North Land (Ateh), the nurses who dwell in the city Pe-Tept (Buto), for they have offered very large offerings in order to cause the child to be made strong for his mother, and to make strong him that is under the knife likewise. Do not allow them to recognize the divine Ka in the Swamp Land, in the city (?) of Nemhettu (?) [and] in her city.'

Then spake Thoth unto the great gods who dwell in the Swamp-Land [saying]: 'O ye nurses who dwell in the city of Pe, who smite [fiends] with your hands, and overthrow [them] with your arms on behalf of that Great One who appeareth in front of you [in] the Sektet Boat, let the Matet (Mantchet) Boat travel on. Horus is to you, he is counted up for life, and he is declared for the life of his father [Osiris]. I have given gladness unto those who are in the Sektet Boat, and the mariners [of Ra] make it to journey on. Horus liveth for his mother Isis and he who is under the knife liveth for his mother likewise. As for the poison, the strength thereof has been made powerless. Verily I am a favoured one, and I will join myself to his hour to hurl back the report of evil to him that sent it forth. The heart of Ra-Heru-Khuti rejoiceth. Thy son Horus is counted up for life [which is] on this child to make him to smite, and to retreat (?) from those who are above, and to turn back the paths of the Sebiu fiends from him, so that he may take possession of the throne of the Two Lands. Ra is in heaven to make answer on behalf of him and his father. The words of power of his mother have lifted up his face, and they protect him and enable him to go round about wheresoever he pleaseth, and to set the terror of him in celestial beings. I have made haste . . .'

HISTORY OF ISIS AND OSIRIS

As told by Plutarch

Translated by E. A. Wallis Budge

This history is taken from the famous treatise of Plutarch entitled *De Iside et Osiride*. Egyptian literature is full of allusions to events which took place in the life of Osiris, and to his persecution, murder, and resurrection, and numerous texts of all periods describe the love and devotion of his sister and wife Isis, and the filial piety of Horus. Nowhere, however, have we in Egyptian a connected account of the causes which led to the murder by Set of Osiris, or of the subsequent events which resulted in his becoming the king of heaven and judge of the dead. However carefully we piece together the fragments of information which we can extract from native Egyptian literature, there still remains a series of gaps which can only be filled by guesswork. Plutarch, as a learned man and a student of comparative religion and mythology was most anxious to understand the history of Isis and Osiris, which Greek and Roman scholars talked about freely, and which none of them comprehended, and he made enquiries of priests and others, and examined critically such information as he could obtain, believing and hoping that he would penetrate the mystery in which these gods were wrapped. As a result of his labours he collected a number of facts about the form of the Legend of Isis and Osiris as it was known to the learned men of his day.

The goddess Rhea, they say, having accompanied with Kronos by stealth, was discovered by Helios who straightway cursed her, and declared that she should not be delivered in any month or year. Hermes, however, being also in love with the same goddess, in return for the favours which he had received from her, went and played at dice with Selene, and won from her the seventieth part of each day. These parts he joined together and made from them five complete days, and he added them to the three hundred and sixty days of which the year formerly consisted. These five days are to this day called the 'Epagomenae', that is, the superadded, and they are observed by them as the birthdays of their gods. On the first of these, they say, Osiris was born, and as he came into the world a voice was heard saying, 'The Lord of All is born.' Some relate the matter in a different way, and say that a certain person named Pamyles, as he was fetching water from the temple of Dios at Thebes, heard a voice commanding him to proclaim aloud that the good and great king Osiris was then born, and that for this reason Kronos committed the education of the child to him, and that in memory of this event the Pamylia were afterwards instituted, which closely resemble the Phallephoria or Priapeia of the Greeks. Upon the second of these days was born Aroueris, whom some call Apollo, and others the Elder Horus. Upon the third day Typhon was born, who came into the world neither at the proper time nor by the right way, but he forced a passage through a wound which he made in his mother's side. Upon the fourth day Isis was born, in the marshes of Egypt, and upon the fifth day Nephthys, whom some call Teleute, or Aphrodite, or Nike, was born. As regards the fathers of these children, the first two are said to have been begotten by Helios, Isis by Hermes, and Typhon and Nephthys by Kronos. Therefore, since the third of the superadded days was the birthday of Typhon, the kings considered it to be unlucky, and in consequence they neither transacted any business in it, nor even suffered themselves to take any refreshment until the evening. They further add that Typhon married Nephthys, and that Isis and Osiris, having a mutual affection, enjoyed each other in their mother's womb before they were born, and that from this commerce sprang Aroueris, whom the Egyptians likewise call Horus the Elder, and the Greeks Apollo.

Osiris having become king of Egypt, applied himself to civilizing his countrymen by turning them from their former indigent and barbarous course of life. He taught them how to cultivate and improve the fruits of the earth, and he gave them a body of laws whereby to regulate their conduct, and instructed them in the reverence and worship which they were to pay to the gods. With the same good disposition he afterwards travelled over the rest of the world, inducing the people everywhere to submit to his discipline, not indeed compelling them by force of arms, but persuading them to yield to the strength of his reasons, which were conveyed to them in the most agreeable manner, in hymns and songs, accompanied with instruments of music. From this last circumstance the Greeks identified him with their Dionysos, or Bacchus. During the absence of Osiris from his kingdom, Typhon had no opportunity of making any innovations in the state, Isis being extremely vigilant in the government, and always upon her guard. After his return, however, having first persuaded seventy-two other people to join with him in the conspiracy, together with a certain queen of Ethiopia called Aso, who chanced to be in Egypt at that time, he formed a crafty plot against him. For having privily taken the measure of the body of Osiris, he caused a chest to be made of exactly the same size, and it was very beautiful and highly decorated. This chest he brought into a certain banqueting room, where it was greatly admired by all who were present, and Typhon, as if in jest, promised to give it to that man whose body when tried would be found to fit it. Thereupon the whole company, one after the other, went into it, but it did not fit any of them; last of all Osiris himself lay down in it. Thereupon all the conspirators ran to the chest, and clapped the cover upon it, and then they fastened it down with nails on the outside, and poured melted lead over it. They next took the chest to the river, which carried it to the sea through the Tanaitic mouth of the Nile; and for this reason this mouth of the Nile is still held in the utmost abomination by the

Egyptians, and is never mentioned by them except with marks of detestation. These things, some say, took place on the seventeenth day of the month of Hathor, when the sun was in Scorpio, in the twenty-eighth year of the reign of Osiris, though others tell us that this was the year of his life and not of his reign.

The first who had knowledge of the accident which had befallen their king were the Pans and Satyrs, who inhabited the country round about Chemmis, and they having informed the people about it, gave the first occasion to the name of Panic Terrors, which has ever since been made use of to signify any sudden fright or amazement of a multitude. As soon as the report reached Isis, she immediately cut off one of the locks of her hair, and put on mourning apparel in that very place where she happened to be; for this reason the place has ever since been called 'Koptos', or the 'city of mourning', though some are of opinion that this word rather signifies 'deprivation'. After this she wandered round about through the country, being full of disquietude and perplexity, searching for the chest, and she inquired of every person she met, including some children whom she saw, whether they knew what was become of it. Now, it so happened that these children had seen what Typhon's accomplices had done with the body, and they accordingly told her by what mouth of the Nile it had been conveyed to the sea. For this reason the Egyptians look upon children as endued with a kind of faculty of divining, and in consequence of this notion are very curious in observing the accidental prattle which they have with one another whilst they are at play, especially if it be in a sacred place, forming omens and presages from it. Isis meanwhile having been informed that Osiris, deceived by her sister Nephthys, who was in love with him, had unwittingly enjoyed her instead of herself, as she concluded from the melilot-garland which he had left with her, made it her business likewise to search out the child, the fruit of this unlawful commerce (for her sister, dreading the anger of her husband Typhon, had exposed it as soon as it was born). Accordingly, after much pain and difficulty, by means of some dogs that conducted her to the place where it was, she found it and bred it up; and in process of time it became her constant guard and attendant, and obtained the name of Anubis, and it is thought that it watches and guards the gods as dogs do men.

At length Isis received more particular news that the chest had been carried by the waves of the sea to the coast of Byblos, and there gently lodged in the branches of a bush of tamarisk, which in a short time had grown up into a large and beautiful tree, and had grown round the chest and enclosed it on every side so completely that it was not to be seen. Moreover, the king of the country, amazed at its unusual size, had cut the tree down, and made that part of the trunk wherein the chest was concealed into a pillar to support the roof of his house. These things, they say, having been made known to Isis in an extraordinary manner by the report of demons, she immediately went to Byblos, where, setting herself down by the side of a fountain, she refused to speak to anybody except the queen's women who chanced to be there. These, however, she saluted and caressed in the kindest manner possible, plaiting their hair for them, and transmitting into them part of that wonderful odour which issued from her own body.

This raised a great desire in the queen their mistress to see the stranger who had this admirable faculty of transfusing so fragrant a smell from herself into the hair and skin of other people. She therefore sent for her to court, and, after a further acquaintance with her, made her nurse to one of her sons. Now, the name of the king who reigned at this time at Byblos was Melkander (Melkarth?), and that of his wife was Astarte, or, according to others, Saôsis, though some call her Nemanoun, which answers to the Greek name Athenais.

Isis nursed the child by giving it her finger to suck instead of the breast. She likewise put him each night into the fire in order to consume his mortal part, whilst, having transformed herself into a swallow, she circled round the pillar and bemoaned her sad fate. This she continued to do for some time, till the queen, who stood watching her, observing the child to be all of a flame, cried out, and thereby deprived him of some of that immortality which would otherwise have been conferred upon him. The goddess then made herself known, and asked that the pillar which supported the roof might be given to her. Having taken the pillar down, she cut it open easily, and having taken out what she wanted, she wrapped up the remainder of the trunk in fine linen, and having poured perfumed oil over it, she delivered it again into the hands of the king and queen. Now, this piece of wood is to this day preserved in the temple, and worshipped by the people of Byblos. When this was done, Isis threw herself upon the chest, and made at the same time such loud and terrible cries of lamentation over it, that the younger of the king's sons who heard her was frightened out of his life. But the elder of them she took with her, and set sail with the chest for Egypt. Now, it being morning the river Phaedrus sent forth a keen and chill air, and becoming angry she dried up its current.

At the first place where she stopped, and when she believed that she was alone, she opened the chest, and laying her face upon that of her dead husband, she embraced him and wept bitterly. Then, seeing that the little boy had silently stolen up behind her, and had found out the reason of her grief, she turned upon him suddenly, and, in her anger, gave him so fierce and terrible a look that he died of fright immediately. Others say that his death did not happen in this manner, but, as already hinted, that he fell into the sea. Afterwards he received the greatest honour on account of the goddess, for this Maneros, whom the Egyptians so frequently call upon at their banquets, is none other than he. This story is contradicted by those who tell us that the true name of this child was Palaestinus, or Pelusius, and that the city of this name was built by the goddess in memory of him. And they further add that this Maneros is thus honoured by the Egyptians at their feasts because he was the first who invented music. Others again state that Maneros is not the name of any particular person, but a customary form of complimentary greeting which the Egyptians use towards each other at their more solemn feasts and banquets, meaning no more by it than to wish 'that what they were then about might prove fortunate and happy to them'. This is the true import of the word. In like manner they say that the human skeleton which is carried about in a box on festal occasions, and shown to the guests, is not designed, as some imagine, to represent the particular misfortunes of Osiris, but rather to remind them of their mortality, and thereby to excite them freely to make use of and to enjoy the good things which are set before them, seeing that they must quickly become such as they there saw. This is the true reason for introducing the skeleton at their banquets. But to proceed with the narrative.

When Isis had come to her son Horus, who was being reared at Buto, she deposited the chest in a remote and unfrequented place. One night, however, when Typhon was hunting by the light of the moon, he came upon it by chance, and recognizing the body which was enclosed in it, he tore it into several pieces, fourteen in all, and scattered them in different places up and down the country. When Isis knew what had been done, she set out in search of the scattered portions of her husband's body; and in order to pass more easily through the lower, marshy parts of the country, she made use of a boat made of the papyrus plant. For this reason, they say, either fearing the anger of the goddess, or else venerating the papyrus, the crocodile never injures anyone who travels in this sort of vessel. And this, they say, hath given rise to the report that there are very many different sepulchres of Osiris in Egypt, for wherever Isis found one of the scattered portions of her husband's body, there she buried it. Others, however, contradict this story, and tell us that the variety of sepulchres of Osiris was due rather to the policy of the queen, who, instead of the real body, as she pretended, presented to these cities only an image of her husband. This she did in order to increase the honours which would by these means be paid to his memory, and also to defeat Typhon, who, if he were victorious in his fight against Horus in which he was about to engage, would search for the body of Osiris, and being distracted by the number of sepulchres would despair of ever being able to find the true one. We are told, moreover, that notwithstanding all her efforts, Isis was never able to discover the phallus of Osiris, which, having been thrown into the Nile immediately upon its separation from the rest of the body, had been devoured by the Lepidotus, the Phagrus, and the Oxyrhynchus, fish which above all others, for this reason, the Egyptians have in more especial avoidance. In order, however, to make some amends for the loss, Isis consecrated the phallus made in imitation of it, and instituted a solemn festival to its memory, which is even to this day observed by the Egyptians.

After these things Osiris returned from the other world, and appeared to his son Horus, and encouraged him to fight, and at the same time instructed him in the exercise of arms. He then asked him what he thought was the most glorious action a man could perform, to which Horus replied, 'To revenge the injuries offered to his father and mother.' Osiris then asked him what animal he thought most serviceable to a soldier, and Horus replied, 'A horse.' On this Osiris wondered, and he questioned him further, asking him why he preferred a horse to a lion, and Horus replied, 'Though the lion is the more serviceable creature to one who stands in need of help, yet is the horse more useful in overtaking and cutting off a flying enemy.' These replies caused Osiris to rejoice greatly, for they showed him that his son was sufficiently prepared for his enemy. We are, moreover, told that amongst the great numbers who were continually deserting from Typhon's party was his concubine Thoueris, and that a serpent which pursued her as she was coming over to Horus was slain by his soldiers. The memory of this action is, they say, still preserved in that cord which is thrown into the midst of their assemblies, and then chopped in pieces. Afterwards a battle took place between Horus and Typhon, which lasted many days, but Horus was at length victorious, and Typhon was taken prisoner. He was delivered over into the custody of Isis, who, instead of putting him to death, loosed his fetters and set him free. This action of his mother incensed Horus to such a degree that he seized her, and pulled the royal crown off her head; but Hermes came forward, and set upon her head the head of an ox instead of a helmet. After this Typhon accused Horus of illegitimacy, but, by the assistance of Hermes, his legitimacy was fully established by a decree of the gods themselves. After this two other battles were fought between Horus and Typhon, and in both Typhon was defeated. Moreover, Isis is said to have had union with Osiris after his death, and she brought forth Harpokrates, who came into the world before his time, and was lame in his lower limbs.

KHNEMU NEFER-HETEP AND THE PRINCESS OF BEKHTEN

Translated by E. A. Wallis Budge

The text of this legend is cut in hieroglyphics upon a sandstone stele, with a rounded top, which was found in the temple of Khensu at Thebes. It was discovered by Champollion in 1846. When the text was first published, and for some years afterwards, it was generally thought that the legend referred to events which were said to have taken place under a king who was identified as Rameses XIII, but this misconception was corrected by Erman, who showed that the king was in reality Rameses II. In fact, the legend was written in the interests of the priests of the temple of Khensu, who wished to magnify their god and his power to cast out devils and to exorcize evil spirits; it was probably composed between 650 BC and 250 BC.

The Horus: 'Mighty Bull, the form (?) of risings, stablished in sovereignty like Tem.' The Golden Horus: 'Mighty one of strength, destroyer of the Nine Nations of the Bow.' King of the South and North: 'The Lord of the Two Lands, User-Maat-Ra-setep-en-Ra Son of Ra: Of his body, Ra-meses-meri-Amen, of Amen-Ra; the Lord of the thrones of the Two Lands, and of the Company of the Gods, the Lords of Thebes, the beloved one. The beneficent god, the son of Amen, born of Mut, begotten of Heru-khuti, the glorious offspring of Neb-tchert, begetting [as] the Bull of his Mother, king of Egypt, Governor of the deserts, the Sovereign who hath taken possession of the Nine Nations of the Bow; [who] on coming forth from the womb ordained mighty things, who gave commands whilst he was in the egg, the Bull, stable of heart, who hath sent forth his seed; the king who is a bull, [and] a god who cometh forth on the day of battle like Menthu, the mighty one of strength like the son of Nut.'

Behold, His Majesty was in the country of Neheru according to his custom every year, and the chiefs of every land, even as far as the swamps, came [to pay] homage, bearing offerings to the Souls of His Majesty; and they brought their gifts, gold, lapis-lazuli, turquoise, bars of wood of every kind of the Land of the God, on their backs, and each one surpassed his neighbour.

And the Prince of Bekhten [also] caused his gifts to be brought, and he set his eldest daughter at the head of them all, and he addressed words of praise to His Majesty, and prayed to him for his life. And the maiden was beautiful, and His Majesty considered her to be the most lovely [woman] in the world, and he wrote down as her title, 'Great Royal Wife, Ra-neferu'; and when His Majesty arrived in Egypt, he did for her whatsoever was done for the Royal Wife.

On the twenty-second day of the second month of the season of Shemu, in the fifteenth year [of his reign], behold, His Majesty was in Thebes, the Mighty [city], the Mistress of cities, performing the praises of Father Amen, the Lord of the thrones of the Two Lands, in his beautiful Festival of the Southern Apt, which was the seat of his heart (i.e., the chosen spot) from primaeval time, [when] one came to say to His Majesty, 'An ambassador of the Prince of Bekhten hath arrived bearing many gifts for the Royal Wife.'

And having been brought into the presence of His Majesty with his gifts, he spake words of adoration to His Majesty, saying, 'Praise be unto thee, O thou Sun (Ra) of the Nine Nations of the Bow, permit us to live before thee!' And when he had spoken, and had smelt the earth before His Majesty, he continued his speech before His Majesty, saying, 'I have come unto thee, my King and Lord, on behalf of Bent-Resht, the younger sister of the Royal Wife Ra-neferu. [Some] disease hath penetrated into her members, and I beseech Thy Majesty to send a man of learning to see her.'

And His Majesty said, 'Bring to me the magicians (or, scribes) of the House of Life, and the nobles of the palace.' And having been brought into his presence straightway, His Majesty said unto them, 'Behold, I have caused you to be summoned [hither] in order that ye may hear this matter. Now bring to me [one] of your company whose heart is wise, and whose fingers are deft.' And the royal scribe Tehuti-em-heb came into the presence of His Majesty, and His Majesty commanded him to depart to Bekhten with that ambassador.

And when the man of learning had arrived in Bekhten, he found Bent-Resht in the condition of a woman who is possessed by a spirit, and he found this spirit to be an evil one, and to be hostile in his disposition towards him.

And the Prince of Bekhten sent a messenger a second time into the presence of His Majesty, saying, 'O King, my Lord, I pray His (i.e., Thy) Majesty to command that a god be brought hither to contend against the spirit.'

Now when the messenger came to His Majesty in the first month of the season of Shemu, in the twenty-sixth year [of his reign], on the day which coincided with that of the Festival of Amen, His Majesty was in the palace (or, temple?) of Thebes. And His Majesty spake a second time in the presence of Khensu in Thebes, [called] 'Nefer-Hetep', saying, 'O my fair Lord, I present myself before thee a second time on behalf of the daughter of the Prince of Bekhten.' Then Khensu, in Thebes, [called] 'Nefer-Hetep', was carried to Khensu, [called] 'Pa-ari-sekher', the great god who driveth away the spirits which attack. And His Majesty spake before Khensu in Thebes, [called] 'Nefer-Hetep', saying, 'O my fair Lord, if thou wilt give (i.e., turn) thy face to Khensu, [called] 'Pa-ari-sekher', the great god who driveth away the spirits which attack, permit thou that he may depart to Bekhten;' [and the god] inclined his head with a deep inclination twice. And His

Majesty said, 'Let, I pray, thy protective (or, magical) power [go] with him, so that I may make His Majesty to go to Bekhten to deliver the daughter of the Prince of Bekhten [from the spirit].'

And Khensu in Thebes, [called] 'Nefer-Hetep', inclined his head with a deep inclination twice. And he made [his] protective power to pass into Khensu, [called] 'Pa-ari-sekher-em-Uast', in a fourfold measure. Then His Majesty commanded that Khensu, [called] 'Pa-ari-sekher-em-Uast', should set out on his journey in a great boat, [accompanied by] five smaller boats, and chariots, and a large number of horses [which marched] on the right side and on the left.

And when this god arrived in Bekhten at the end of a period of one year and five months, the Prince of Bekhten came forth with his soldiers and his chief[s] before Khensu, [called] 'Pa-ari-sekher', and he cast himself down upon his belly, saying, 'Thou hast come to us, and thou art welcomed by us, by the commands of the King of the South and North, User-Maat-Ra-setep-en-Ra!'

And when this god had passed over to the place where Bent-Resht was, he worked upon the daughter of the Prince of Bekhten with his magical power, and she became better (i.e., was healed) straightway. And this spirit which had been with her said, in the presence of Khensu, [called] 'Pa-ari-sekher-em-Uast', 'Come in peace (i.e., Welcome!), O great god, who dost drive away the spirits which attack! Bekhten is thy city, the people thereof, both men and women, are thy servants, and I myself am thy servant. I will [now] depart unto the place whence I came, so that I may cause thy heart to be content about the matter concerning which thou hast come. I pray that Thy Majesty will command that a happy day (i.e., a festival, or day of rejoicing) be made with me, and with the Prince of Bekhten.' And this god inclined his head [in approval] to his priest, saying, 'Let the Prince of Bekhten make a great offering in the presence of this spirit.'

Now whilst Khensu, [called] 'Pa-ari-sekher-em-Uast', was arranging these [things] with the spirit, the Prince of Bekhten and his soldiers were standing there, and they feared with an exceedingly great fear. And the Prince of Bekhten made a great offering in the presence of Khensu, [called] 'Pa-ari-sekher-em-Uast', and the spirit of the Prince of Bekhten, and he made a happy day (i.e., festival) on their behalf, and [then] the spirit departed in peace unto the place which he loved, by the command of Khensu, [called] 'Pa-ari-sekher-em-Uast'. And the Prince of Bekhten, and every person who was in the country of Bekhten, rejoiced very greatly, and he took counsel with his heart, saying, 'It hath happened that this god hath been given as a gift to Bekhten, and I will not permit him to depart to Egypt.'

And [when] this god had tarried for three years and nine months in Bekhten, the Prince of Bekhten, who was lying down asleep on his bed, saw this god come forth outside his shrine (now he was in the form of a golden hawk), and he flew up into the heavens and departed to Egypt; and when the Prince woke up he was trembling. And he said unto the prophet of Khensu, [called] 'Pa-ari-sekher-em-Uast', 'This god who tarried with us hath departed to Egypt; let his chariot also depart to Egypt.'

And the Prince of Bekhten permitted [the image of] the god

to set out for Egypt, and he gave him many great gifts of beautiful things of all kinds, and a large number of soldiers and horses [went with him]. And when they had arrived in peace in Thebes, Khensu, [called] 'Pa-ari-sekher-em-Uast', went into the Temple of Khensu in Thebes, [called] 'Nefer-Hetep', and he placed the offerings which the Prince of Bekhten had given unto him, beautiful things of all kinds, before Khensu in Thebes, [called] 'Nefer-Hetep', and he gave nothing thereof whatsoever to his [own] temple.

Thus Khensu, [called] 'Pa-ari-sekher-em-Uast', arrived in his temple in peace, on the nineteenth day of the second month of the season Pert, in the thirty-third year of the [reign of the] King of the South and North, User-Maat-en-Ra-setep-en-Ra, the giver of life, like Ra, for ever.

KHNEMU AND THE SEVEN YEARS' FAMINE

Translated by E. A. Wallis Budge

The text of this most interesting legend is found in hieroglyphics on one side of a large rounded block of granite some eight or nine feet high, which stands on the south-east portion of Sahal, a little island lying in the First Cataract, two or three miles to the south of Elephantine Island and the modern town of Aswan. The legend contained in this remarkable text describes a terrible famine which took place in the reign of Tcheser, a king of the IIIrd Dynasty, and lasted for seven years. Insufficient Nile-floods were, of course, the physical cause of the famine, but the legend shows that the 'low Niles' were brought about by the neglect of the Egyptians in respect of the worship of the god of the First Cataract, the great god Khnemu.

In the eighteenth year of the Horus, Neter-Khat, of the King of the South and North, Neter-Khat, of the Lord of the Shrines of Uatchit and Nekhebit, Neter-Khat, of the Golden Horus Tcheser, when Matar was Ha Prince, and Erpa, and Governor of the temple-cities in the Land of the South, and director of the Khenti folk in Abtu, there was brought unto him the following royal despatch: 'This is to inform thee that misery hath laid hold upon me [as I sit] upon the great throne by reason of those who dwell in the Great House. My heart is grievously afflicted by reason of the exceedingly great evil [which hath happened] because Hapi (i.e., the Nile) hath not come forth in my time to the [proper] height for seven years. Grain is very scarce, vegetables are lacking altogether, every kind of thing which men eat for their food hath ceased, and every man [now] plundereth his neighbour. Men wish to walk, but are unable to move, the child waileth, the young man draggeth his limbs along, and the hearts of the aged folk are crushed with despair; their legs give way under them, and they sink down to the ground, and their hands are laid upon their bodies [in pain]. The shennu nobles are destitute of counsel, and [when] the storehouses which should contain supplies are opened, there cometh forth therefrom nothing but wind. Everything is in a state of ruin. My mind hath remembered, going back to former time, when I had an advocate, to the time of the gods, and of the Ibis-god, and of the chief Kher-heb priest I-em-hetep, the son of Ptah of his Southern Wall.'

'Where is the place of birth of Hapi (the Nile)? What god, or what goddess, presideth (?) over it? What manner of form hath he? It is he who stablisheth revenue for me, and a full store of grain. I would go to the Chief of Het-Sekhet whose beneficence strengtheneth all men in their works. I would enter into the House of Life, I would unfold the written rolls [therein], and I would lay my hand upon them.'

Then [Matar] set out on his journey, and he returned to me straightway. He gave me instruction concerning the increase of Hapi, and told me all things which men had written concerning it, and he revealed to me the secret doors (?) whereto my ancestors had betaken themselves quickly, the like of which has never been, to [any] king since the time of Ra (?). And he said unto me: 'There is a city in the middle of the stream wherefrom Hapi maketh his appearance; "Abu" was its name in the beginning; it is the City of the Beginning, and it is the Nome of the City of the Beginning. [It reacheth] to Uaua, which is the beginning of the land. There is too a flight of steps, which reareth itself to a great height, and is the support of Ra, when he maketh his calculation to prolong life to everyone; "Netchemtchem Ankh" is the name of its abode. "The two Qerti" is the name of the water, and they are the two breasts from which every good thing cometh forth (?).

'Here is the bed of Hapi (the Nile), wherein he reneweth his youth [in his season], wherein he causeth the flooding of the land. He cometh and hath union as he journeyeth, as a man hath union with a woman. And again he playeth the part of a husband and satisfieth his desire. He riseth to the height of twenty-eight cubits [at Abu], and he droppeth at Sma-Behutet to seven cubits. The union (?) there is that of the god Khnemu in

[Abu. He smiteth the ground] with his sandals, and [its] fulness becometh abundant; he openeth the bolt of the door with his hand, and he throweth open the double door of the opening through which the water cometh.

'Moreover, he dwelleth there in the form of the god Shu, as one who is lord over his own territory, and his homestead, the name of which is "Aa" (i.e., the "Island"). There he keepeth an account of the products of the Land of the South and of the Land of the North, in order to give unto every god his proper share, and he leadeth to each [the metals], and the [precious stones, and the four-footed beasts], and the feathered fowl, and the fish, and every thing whereon they live. And the cord [for the measuring of the land] and the tablet whereon the register is kept are there.

'And there is an edifice of wood there, with the portals thereof formed of reeds, wherein he dwelleth as one who is over his own territory, and he maketh the foliage of the trees (?) to serve as a roof.

'His God-house hath an opening towards the south-east, and Ra (or, the Sun) standeth immediately opposite thereto every day. The stream which floweth along the south side thereof hath danger [for him that attacketh it], and it hath as a defence a wall which entereth into the region of the men of Kens on the South. Huge mountains [filled with] masses of stone are round about its domain on the east side, and shut it in. Thither come the quarrymen with things (tools?) of every kind, [when] they seek to build a House for any god in the Land of the South, or in the Land of the North, or [shrines] as abodes for sacred animals, or royal pyramids, and statues of all kinds. They stand up in front of the House of the God and in the sanctuary chamber, and their sweet smelling offerings are presented before the face of the god Khnemu during his circuit, even as [when they bring] garden herbs and flowers of every kind. The fore parts thereof are in Abu (Elephantine), and the hind parts are in the city of Sunt (?). One portion thereof is on the east side of the river, and another portion is on the west side of the river, and another portion is in the middle of the river. The stream decketh the region with its waters during a certain season of the year, and it is a place of delight for every man. And works are carried on among these quarries [which are] on the edges [of the river?], for the stream immediately faceth this city of Abu itself, and there existeth the granite, the substance whereof is hard (?); "Stone of Abu" it is called.

'[Here is] a list of the names of the gods who dwell in the Divine House of Khnemu. The goddess of the star Sept (Sothis), the goddess Anqet, Hap (the Nile-god), Shu, Keb, Nut, Osiris, Horus, Isis, and Nephthys.

'[Here are] the names of the stones which lie in the heart of the mountains, some on the east side, some on the west side, and some in [the midst of] the stream of Abu. They exist in the heart of Abu, they exist in the country on the east bank, and in the country on the west bank, and in the midst of the stream, namely, Bekhen-stone, Meri (or Meli)-stone, Atbekhab (?)-stone, Rakes-stone, and white Utshi-stone; these are found on the east bank. Per-tchani-stone is found on the west bank, and the Teshi-stone in the river.

'[Here are] the names of the hard (or, hidden) precious stones, which are found in the upper side, among them being the . . . stone, the name of which hath spread abroad through [a space of] four atru measures: Gold, Silver, Copper, Iron, Lapis-lazuli, Emerald, Thehen (Crystal?), Khenem (Ruby), Kai, Mennu, Betka (?), Temi, Na (?). The following come forth from the fore part of the land: Mehi-stone, [He]maki-stone, Abheti-stone, iron ore, alabaster for statues, mother-of-emerald, antimony, seeds (or, gum) of the sehi plant, seeds (or, gum) of the amem plant, and seeds (or, gum) of the incense plant; these are found in the fore parts of its double city.' These were the things which I learned therefrom (i.e., from Matar).

Now my heart was very happy when I heard these things, and I entered into [the temple of Khnemu]. The overseers unrolled the documents which were fastened up, the water of purification was sprinkled [upon me], a progress was made [through] the secret places, and a great offering [consisting] of bread-cakes, beer, geese, oxen (or, bulls), and beautiful things of all kinds were offered to the gods and goddesses who dwell in Abu, whose names are proclaimed at the place [which is called], 'Couch of the heart in life and power.'

And I found the God standing in front of me, and I made him to be at peace with me by means of the thank-offering which I offered unto him, and I made prayer and supplication before him. Then he opened his eyes, and his heart was inclined [to hear] me, and his words were strong [when he said], 'I am Khnemu, who fashioned thee. My two hands were about thee and knitted together thy body, and made healthy thy members; and it is I who gave thee thy heart. Yet the minerals (or, precious stones) [lie] under each other, [and they have done so] from olden time, and no man hath worked them in order to build the houses of the god, or to restore those which have fallen into ruin, or to hew out shrines for the gods of the South and of the North, or to do what he ought to do for his lord, notwithstanding that I am the Lord and the Creator.

'I am [he] who created himself, Nu, the Great [God], who came into being at the beginning, [and] Hapi, who riseth according to his will, in order to give health to him that laboureth for me. I am the Director and Guide of all men at their seasons, the Most Great, the Father of the Gods, Shu, the Great One, the Chief of the Earth. The two halves of the sky (i.e., the East and the West) are as a habitation below me. A lake of water hath been poured out for me, [namely,] Hap (i.e., the Nile), which embraceth the field-land, and his embrace provideth the [means of] life for every nose (i.e., every one), according to the extent of his embrace of the field-land. With old age [cometh] the condition of weakness. I will make Hap (i.e., the Nile) rise for thee, and [in] no year shall [he] fail, and he shall spread himself out in rest upon every land. Green plants and herbs and trees shall bow beneath [the weight of] their produce. The goddess Renenet shall be at the head of everything, and every product shall increase by hundreds of thousands, according to the cubit of the year. The people shall be filled, verily to their hearts' desire, and everyone. Misery shall pass away, and the emptiness of their storehouses of grain shall come to an end. The land of Ta-Mert (i.e., Egypt) shall come to be a region of cultivated land, the districts [thereof] shall be yellow with grain crops, and the grain [thereof] shall be goodly. And fertility shall come according to the desire [of the people], more than there hath ever been before.'

Then I woke up at [the mention of] crops, my heart (or, courage) came [back], and was equal to my [former] despair, and I made the following decree in the temple of my father Khnemu:

'The king giveth an offering to Khnemu the Lord of the city of Qebhet, the Governor of Ta-Sti, in return for those things which thou hast done for me. There shall be given unto thee on thy right hand [the river bank] of Manu, and on thy left hand the river bank of Abu, together with the land about the city, for a space of twenty measures, on the east side and on the west side, with the gardens, and the river front everywhere throughout the region included in these measures. From every husbandman who tilleth the ground, and maketh to live again the slain, and placeth water upon the river banks and all the islands which are in front of the region of these measures, shall be demanded a further contribution from the growing crops and from every storehouse, as thy share.

'Whatsoever is caught in the nets by every fisherman and by every fowler, and whatsoever is taken by the catchers of fish, and by the snarers of birds, and by every hunter of wild animals, and by every man who snareth lions in the mountains, when these things enter [the city] one tenth of them shall be demanded.

'And of all the calves which are cast throughout the regions which are included in these measures, one tenth of their number shall be set apart as animals which are sealed for all the burnt offerings which are offered up daily.

'And, moreover, the gift of one tenth shall be levied upon the gold, ivory, ebony, spices, carnelians (?), sa wood, seshes spice, dum palm fruit (?), nef wood, and upon woods and products of every kind whatsoever, which the Khentiu, and the Khentiu of Hen-Resu, and the Egyptians, and every person whatsoever [shall bring in].

'And [every] hand shall pass them by, and no officer of the revenue whatsoever shall utter a word beyond these places to demand (or, levy on) things from them, or to take things over and above [those which are intended for] thy capital city.

'And I will give unto thee the land belonging to the city, which beareth stones, and good land for cultivation. Nothing thereof shall be [diminished] or withheld, of all these things in order to deceive the scribes, and the revenue officers, and the inspectors of the king, on whom it shall be incumbent to certify everything.

'And further, I will cause the masons, and the hewers of ore (?), and the workers in metal, and the smelters (?) of gold, and the sculptors in stone, and the ore-crushers, and the furnace-men (?), and handicraftsmen of every kind whatsoever, who work in hewing, and cutting, and polishing these stones, and in gold, and silver, and copper, and lead, and every worker in wood who shall cut down any tree, or carry on a trade of any kind, or work which is connected with the wood trade, to pay tithe upon all the natural products (?), and also upon the hard stones which are brought from their beds above, and quarried stones of all kinds.

'And there shall be an inspector over the weighing of the gold, and silver, and copper, and real (i.e., precious) stones, and the [other] things, which the metal-workers require for the House of Gold, and the sculptors of the images of the gods need in the making and repairing of them, and [these things] shall be exempted from tithing, and the workmen also. And everything shall be delivered (or, given) in front of the storehouse to their children, a second time, for the protection of everything. And whatsoever is before thy God-house shall be in abundance, just as it hath ever been from the earliest time.

'And a copy of this decree shall be inscribed upon a stele, [which shall be set up] in the holy place, according to the writing of the [original] document which is cut upon wood, and [figures of] this god and the overseers of the temple shall be [cut] thereon. Whosoever shall spit upon that which is on it shall be admonished by the rope. And the overseers of the priests, and every overseer of the people of the House of the God, shall ensure the perpetuation of my name in the House of the god Khnemu-Ra, the lord of Abu (Elephantine), for ever.'

THE STORY OF SANEHAT

Translated by E. A. Wallis Budge

The text of this very interesting story is found written in the hieratic character upon papyri which are preserved in Berlin. The narrative describes events which are said to have taken place under one of the kings of the XIIth Dynasty, and it is very possible that the foundation of this story is historical. The hero is himself supposed to relate his own adventures.

The Erpā, the Duke, the Chancellor of the King of the North, the smer uati, the judge, the Āntchmer of the marches, the King in the lands of the Nubians, the veritable royal kinsman loving him, the member of the royal bodyguard, Sanehat, saith: I am a member of the bodyguard of his lord, the servant of the King, and of the house of Neferit, the feudal chieftainess, the Erpāt princess, the highly favoured lady, the royal wife of Usertsen, whose word is truth in Khnemetast, the royal daughter of Amenemhāt, whose word is truth in Qanefer. On the seventh day of the third month of the season Akhet, in the thirtieth year [of his reign], the god drew nigh to his horizon, and the King of the South, the King of the North, SehetepabRa, ascended into heaven, and was invited to the Disk, and his divine members mingled with those of him that made him. The King's House was in silence, hearts were bowed down in sorrow, the two Great Gates were shut fast, the officials sat motionless, and the people mourned.

Now behold [before his death] His Majesty had despatched an army to the Land of the Themehu, under the command of his eldest son, the beautiful god Usertsen. And he went and raided the desert lands in the south, and captured slaves from the Thehenu (Libyans), and he was at that moment returning and bringing back Libyan slaves and innumerable beasts of every kind. And the high officers of the Palace sent messengers into the western country to inform the King's son concerning what had taken place in the royal abode. And the messengers found him on the road, and they came to him by night and asked him if it was not the proper time for him to hasten his return, and to set out with his bodyguard without letting his army in general know of his departure. They also told him that a message had been sent to the princes who were in command of the soldiers in his train not to proclaim [the matter of the King's death] to any one else.

Sanehat continues: When I heard his voice speaking I rose up and fled. My heart was cleft in twain, my arms dropped by my side, and trembling seized all my limbs. I ran about distractedly, hither and thither, seeking a hiding-place. I went into the thickets in order to find a place wherein I could travel without being seen. I made my way upstream, and I decided not to appear in the Palace, for I did not know but that deeds of violence were taking place there. And I did not say, 'Let life follow it,' but I went on my way to the district of the Sycamore. Then I came to the Lake (or Island) of Seneferu, and I passed the whole day there on the edge of the plain. On the following morning I continued my journey, and a man rose up immediately in front of me on the road, and he cried for mercy; he was afraid of me. When the night fell I walked into the village of Nekau, and I crossed the river in an usekht boat without a rudder, by the help of the wind from the west. And I travelled eastwards of the district of Aku, by the pass of the goddess Herit, the Lady of the Red Mountain. Then I allowed my feet to take the road downstream, and I travelled on to Anebuheq, the fortress that had been built to drive back the Satiu (nomad marauders), and to hold in check the tribes that roamed the desert. I crouched down in the scrub during the day to avoid being seen by the watchmen on the top of the fortress. I set out again on the march, when the night fell, and when daylight fell on the earth I arrived at Peten, and I rested myself by the Lake of Kamur. Then thirst came upon me and overwhelmed me. I suffered torture. My throat was burnt up, and I said, 'This indeed is the taste of death.' But I took courage, and collected my members (i.e. myself), for I heard the sounds that are made by flocks and herds. Then the Satiu of the desert saw me, and the master of the caravan who had been in Egypt recognized me. And he rose up and gave me some water, and he warmed milk [for me], and I travelled with the men of his caravan, and thus I passed through one country after the other [in safety]. I avoided the land of Sunu and I journeyed to the land of Qetem, where I stayed for a year and a half.

And Āmmuiansha, the Shēkh of Upper Thennu, took me aside and said unto me, 'Thou wilt be happy with me, for thou wilt hear the language of Egypt.' Now he said this because he knew what manner of man I was, for he had heard the people of Egypt who were there with him bear testimony concerning my character. And he said unto me, 'Why and wherefore hast thou come hither? Is it because the departure of King SehetepabRa from the Palace to the horizon hath taken place, and thou didst not know what would be the result of it?' Then I spake unto him with words of deceit, saying, 'I was among the soldiers who had gone to the land of Themeh. My heart cried out, my courage failed me utterly, it made me follow the ways over which I fled. I hesitated, but felt no regret. I did not hearken unto any evil counsel, and my name was not heard on the mouth of the herald. How I came to be brought into this country I know not; it was, perhaps, by the Providence of God.'

And Āmmuiansha said unto me, 'What will become of the land without that beneficent god the terror of whom passed through the lands like the goddess Sekhmet in a year of pestilence?' Then I made answer unto him, saying, 'His son shall save us. He hath entered the Palace, and hath taken possession of the heritage of his father. Moreover, he is the god who hath no equal, and no other can exist beside him, the lord of wisdom, perfect in his plans, of good will when he passeth decrees, and one cometh forth and goeth in according to his ordinance. He reduced foreign lands to submission whilst his father [sat] in the Palace directing him in the matters which had to be carried out. He is mighty of valour, he slayeth with his sword, and in bravery he hath no compeer. One should see him attacking the nomads of the desert, and pouncing upon the robbers of the highway! He beateth down opposition, he smiteth arms helpless, his enemies cannot be made to resist him. He taketh vengeance, he cleaveth skulls, none can stand up before him. His strides are long, he slayeth him that fleeth, and he who turneth his back upon him in flight never reacheth his goal. When attacked his courage standeth firm. He attacketh again and again, and he never yieldeth. His heart is bold when he seeth the battle array, he permitteth none to sit down behind. His face is fierce [as] he rusheth on the attacker. He rejoiceth when he taketh captive the chief of a band of desert robbers. He seizeth his shield, he raineth blows upon him, but he hath no need to repeat his attack, for he slayeth his foe before he can hurl his spear at him. Before he draweth his bow the nomads have fled, his arms are like the souls of the Great Goddess. He fighteth, and if he reacheth his object of attack he spareth not, and he leaveth no remnant. He is beloved, his pleasantness is great, he is the conqueror, and his town loveth him more than herself; she rejoiceth in him more than in her god, and men throng about him with rejoicings. He was king and conqueror before his birth, and he hath worn his crowns since he was born. He hath multiplied births, and he it is whom God hath made to be the joy of this land, which he hath ruled, and the boundaries of which he hath enlarged. He hath conquered the Lands of the South, shall he not conquer the Lands of the North? He hath been created to smite the hunters of the desert, and to crush the tribes that roam the sandy waste....' Then the Shēkh of Upper Thennu said unto me, 'Assuredly Egypt is a happy country in that it knoweth his vigour. Verily, as long as thou tarriest with me I will do good unto thee.'

And he set me before his children, and he gave me his eldest daughter to wife, and he made me to choose for myself a very fine territory which belonged to him, and which lay on the border of a neighbouring country, and this beautiful region was called Aa. In it there are figs, and wine is more abundant than water. Honey is plentiful, oil existeth in large quantities, and fruits of every kind are on the trees thereof. Wheat, barley, herds of cattle, and flocks of sheep and goats are there in untold numbers. And the Shēkh showed me very great favour, and his affection for me was so great that he made me Shēkh of one of the best tribes in his country. Bread-cakes were made for me each day, and each day wine was brought to me with roasted flesh and wild fowl, and the wild creatures of the plain that were caught were laid before me, in addition to the game which my hunting dogs brought in. Food of all kinds was made for me, and milk was prepared for me in various ways. I passed many years in this manner, and my children grew up into fine strong men, and each one of them ruled his tribe. Every ambassador on his journey to and from Egypt visited me. I was kind to people of every class. I gave water to the thirsty man. I suppressed the highway robber. I directed the operations of the bowmen of the desert, who marched long distances to suppress the hostile Shēkhs, and to reduce their power, for the Shēkh of Thennu had appointed me General of his soldiers many years before this. Every country against which I marched I terrified into submission. I seized the crops by the wells, I looted the flocks and herds, I carried away the people and their slaves who ate their bread, I slew the men there. Through my sword and bow, and through my well-organised campaigns, I was highly esteemed in the mind of the Shēkh, and he loved me, for he knew my bravery, and he set me before his children when he saw the bravery of my arms.

Then a certain mighty man of valour of Thennu came and reviled me in my tent; he was greatly renowned as a man of war, and he was unequalled in the whole country, which he had conquered. He challenged me to combat, being urged to fight by the men of his tribe, and he believed that he could conquer me, and he determined to take my flocks and herds as spoil. And the Shēkh took counsel with me about the challenge, and I said, 'I am not an acquaintance of his, and I am by no means a friend of his. Have I ever visited him in his domain or entered his door, or passed through his compound? [Never!] He is a man whose heart becometh full of evil thoughts, whensoever he seeth me, and he wisheth to carry out his fell design and plunder me. He is like a wild bull seeking to slay the bull of a herd of tame cattle so that he may make the cows his own. Or rather he is a mere braggart who wisheth to seize the property which I have collected by my prudence, and not an experienced warrior. Or rather he is a bull that loveth to fight, and that loveth to make attacks repeatedly, fearing that otherwise some other animal will prove to be his equal. If, however, his heart be set upon fighting, let him declare [to me] his intention. Is God, Who knoweth everything, ignorant of what he hath decided to do?'

And I passed the night in stringing my bow, I made ready my arrows of war, I unsheathed my dagger, and I put all my weapons in order. At daybreak the tribes of the land of Thennu came, and the people who lived on both sides of it gathered themselves together, for they were greatly concerned about the combat, and they came and stood up round about me where I stood. Every heart burned for my success, and both men and women uttered cries (or exclamations), and every heart suffered anxiety on my behalf, saying, 'Can there exist possibly any man who is a mightier fighter and more doughty as a man of war than he?' Then mine adversary grasped his shield, and his battle-axe, and his spears, and after he had hurled his weapons at me, and I had succeeded in avoiding his short spears, which arrived harmlessly one after the other, he became filled with fury, and making up his mind to attack me at close quarters he threw himself upon me. And I hurled my javelin at him, which remained fast in his neck, and he uttered a long cry and fell on his face, and I slew him with his own weapons. And as I stood upon his back I shouted the cry of victory, and every Āamu man (i.e. Asiatic) applauded me, and I gave thanks to Menthu; and the slaves of my opponent mourned for their lord. And the Shēkh Āmmuiansha took me in his arms and embraced me. I carried off his (i.e. the opponent's) property. I seized his cattle as spoil, and what he meditated doing to me I did unto him. I took possession of the contents of his tent, I stripped his compound, I became rich, I increased my store of goods, and I added greatly to the number of my cattle.

Thus did God prosper the man who made Him his support. Thus that day was washed (i.e. satisfied) the heart of the man who was compelled to make his escape from his own into another country. Thus that day the integrity of the man who was once obliged to take to flight as a miserable fugitive was proven in the sight of all the Court. Once I was a wanderer wandering about hungry, and now I can give bread to my neighbours. Once I had to flee naked from my country, and now I am the possessor of splendid raiment, and of apparel made of the finest byssus. Once I was obliged to do my own errands and to fetch and carry for myself, and now I am the master of troops of servants. My house is beautiful, my estate is spacious, and my name is repeated in the Great House. O Lord of the gods, who hath ordered my goings, I will offer propitiatory offerings unto Thee: I beseech Thee to restore me to Egypt, and O be Thou pleased most graciously to let me once again look upon the spot where my mind dwelleth for hours [at a time]! How great a boon would it be for me to cleanse my body in the land of my birth! Let, I pray, a period of happiness attend me, and may God give me peace. May He dispose events in such a way that the close of the career of the man who hath suffered misery, whose heart hath seen sorrow, who hath wandered into a strange land, may be happy. Is He not at peace with me this day? Surely He shall hearken to him that is afar off.... Let the King of Egypt be at peace with me, and may I live upon his offerings. Let me salute the Mistress of the Land (i.e. the Queen) who is in his palace, and let me hear the greetings of her children. O would that my members could become young again! For now old age is stealing on me. Infirmity overtaketh me. Mine eyes refuse to see, my hands fall helpless, my knees shake, my heart standeth still, the funerary mourners approach and they will bear me away to the City of Eternity, wherein I shall become a follower of Nebertcher. She will declare to me the beauties of her children, and they shall traverse it with me.

Behold now, the Majesty of the King of Egypt, KheperkaRa, whose word is truth, having spoken concerning the various things that had happened to me, sent a messenger to me bearing royal gifts, such as he would send to the king of a foreign land, with the intention of making glad the heart of thy servant now [speaking], and the princes of his palace made me to hear their salutations. And here is a copy of the document, which was brought to thy servant [from the King] instructing him to return to Egypt.

'The royal command of the Horus, Ānkh-mestu, Lord of Nekhebet and Uatchet, Ānkh-mestu, King of the South, King of the North, KheperkaRa, the son of Ra, Amenemhāt, the everliving, to my follower Sanehat. This royal order is despatched unto thee to inform thee. Thou hast travelled about everywhere, in one country after another, having set out from Qetem and reached Thennu, and thou hast journeyed from place to place at thine own will and pleasure. Observe now, what thou hast done [unto others, making them to obey thee], shall be done unto thee. Make no excuses, for they shall be set aside; argue not with [my] officials, for thy arguments shall be refuted. Thy heart shall not reject the plans which thy mind hath formulated. Thy Heaven (i.e. the Queen), who is in the Palace, is stable and flourishing at this present time, her head is crowned with the sovereignty of the earth, and her children are in the royal chambers of the Palace. Lay aside the honours which thou hast, and thy life of abundance (or luxury), and journey to Egypt. Come and look upon thy native land, the land where thou wast born, smell the earth (i.e. do homage) before the Great Gate, and associate with the nobles thereof. For at this time thou art beginning to be an old man, and thou canst no longer produce sons, and thou hast [ever] in thy mind the day of [thy] burial, when thou wilt assume the form of a servant [of Osiris]. The unguents for thine embalmment on the night [of mummification] have been set apart for thee, together with thy mummy swathings, which are the work of the hands of the goddess Tait. Thy funerary procession, which will march on the day of thy union with the earth, hath been arranged, and there are prepared for thee a gilded mummy-case, the head whereof is painted blue, and a canopy made of mesket wood. Oxen shall draw thee [to the tomb], the wailing women shall precede thee, the funerary dances shall be performed, those who mourn thee shall be at the door of thy tomb, the funerary offerings dedicated to thee shall be proclaimed, sacrifices shall be offered for thee with thy oblations, and thy funerary edifice shall be built in white stone, side by side with those of the princes and princesses. Thy death must not take place in a foreign land, the Āamu folk shall not escort thee [to thy grave], thou shalt not be placed in the skin of a ram when thy burial is effected; but at thy burial there shall be ... and the smiting of the earth, and when thou departest lamentations shall be made over thy body.'

When this royal letter reached me I was standing among the people of my tribe, and when it had been read to me I threw myself face downwards on the ground, and bowed until my head touched the dust, and I clasped the document reverently to my breast. Then [I rose up] and walked to and fro in my abode, rejoicing and saying, 'How can these things possibly be done to thy servant who is now speaking, whose heart made him to fly into foreign lands [where dwell] peoples who stammer in their speech? Assuredly it is a good and gracious thought [of the King] to deliver me from death [here], for thy Ka (i.e. double) will make my body to end [its existence] in my native land.'

Here is a copy of the reply that was made by the servant of the Palace, Sanehat, to the above royal document:

'In peace the most beautiful and greatest! Thy Ka knoweth of the flight which thy servant, who is now speaking, made when he was in a state of ignorance, O thou beautiful god, Lord of Egypt, beloved of Ra, favoured of Menthu, the Lord of Thebes. May Amen-Ra, lord of the thrones of the Two Lands, and Sebek, and Ra, and Horus, and Hathor, and Tem and his Company of the Gods, and Neferbaiu, and Semsuu, and Horus of the East, and Nebt-Amehet, the goddess who is joined to thy head, and the

Tchatchau gods who preside over the Nile flood, and Menu, and Heru-khenti-semti, and Urrit, the Lady of Punt, and Nut, and Heru-ur (Haroeris), and Ra, and all the gods of Tamera (Egypt), and of the Islands of the Great Green Sea (i.e. Mediterranean), bestow upon thee a full measure of their good gifts, and grant life and serenity to thy nostrils, and may they grant unto thee an eternity which hath no limit, and everlastingness which hath no bounds! May thy fear penetrate and extend into all countries and mountains, and mayest thou be the possessor of all the region which the sun encircleth in his course. This is the prayer which thy servant who now speaketh maketh on behalf of his lord who hath delivered him from Ament.

'The lord of knowledge who knoweth men, the Majesty of the Setepsa abode (i.e. the Palace), knoweth well that his servant who is now speaking was afraid to declare the matter, and that to repeat it was a great thing. The great god (i.e. the King), who is the counterpart of Ra, hath done wisely in what he hath done, and thy servant who now speaketh hath meditated upon it in his mind, and hath made himself to conform to his plans. Thy Majesty is like unto Horus, and the victorious might of thine arms hath conquered the whole world. Let thy Majesty command that Maka [chief of] the country of Qetma, and Khentiaaush [chief of] Khent-Keshu, and Menus [chief of] the lands of the Fenkhu, be brought hither, and these Governors will testify that these things have come to pass at the desire of thy Ka (i.e. double), and that Thenu doth not speak words of overboldness to thee, and that she is as [obedient as] thy hunting dogs. Behold, the flight, which thy servant who is now speaking made, was made by him as the result of ignorance; it was not wilful, and I did not decide upon it after careful meditation. I cannot understand how I could ever have separated myself from my country. It seemeth to me now to have been the product of a dream wherein a man who is in the swamps of the Delta imagineth himself to be in Abu (Elephantine, or Syene), or of a man who whilst standing in fertile fields imagineth himself to be in the deserts of the Sūdān. I fear nothing and no man can make with truth [accusations] against me. I have never turned my ear to disloyal plottings, and my name hath never been in the mouth of the crier [of the names of proscribed folk]; though my members quaked, and my legs shook, my heart guided me, and the God who ordained this flight of mine led me on. Behold, I am not a stiff-necked man (or rebel), nay, I held in honour [the King], for I knew the land of Egypt and that Ra hath made thy fear to exist everywhere in Egypt, and the awe of thee to permeate every foreign land. I beseech thee to let me enter my native land. I beseech thee to let me return to Egypt. Thou art the apparel of the horizon. The Disk (i.e. the sun) shineth at thy wish. One drinketh the water of the river Nile at thy pleasure. One breatheth the air of heaven when thou givest the word of command. Thy servant who now speaketh will transfer the possessions which he hath gotten in this land to his kinsfolk. And as for the embassy of thy Majesty which hath been despatched to the servant who now speaketh, I will do according to thy Majesty's desire, for I live by the breath which thou givest, O thou beloved of Ra, Horus, and Hathor, and thy holy nostrils are beloved of Menthu, Lord of Thebes; mayest thou live for ever!'

And I tarried one day in the country of Aa in order to transfer my possessions to my children. My eldest son attended to the affairs of the people of my settlement, and the men and women thereof (i.e. the slaves), and all my possessions were in his hand, and all my children, and all my cattle, and all my fruit trees, and all my palm plantations and groves. Then thy servant who is now speaking set out on his journey and travelled towards the South. When I arrived at Heruuatu, the captain of the frontier patrol sent a messenger to inform the Court of my arrival. His Majesty sent a courteous overseer of the servants of the Palace, and following him came large boats laden with gifts from the King for the soldiers of the desert who had escorted me and guided me to the town of Heruuatu. I addressed each man among them by name and every toiler had that which belonged to him. I continued my journey, the wind bore me along, food was prepared for me and drink made ready for me, and the best of apparel (?), until I arrived at Athettaui. On the morning of the day following my arrival, five officials came to me, and they bore me to the Great House, and I bowed low until my forehead touched the ground before him. And the princes and princesses were standing waiting for me in the umtet chamber, and they advanced to meet me and to receive me, and the smeru officials conducted me into the hall, and led me to the privy chamber of the King, where I found His Majesty [seated] upon the Great Throne in the umtet chamber of silver-gold. I arrived there, I raised myself up after my prostrations, and I knew not that I was in his presence. Then this god (i.e. the King) spake unto me harshly, and I became like unto a man who is confounded in the darkness; my intelligence left me, my limbs quaked, my heart was no longer in my body, and I knew not whether I was dead or alive. Then His Majesty said unto one of his high officials, 'Raise him, and let him speak unto me.' And His Majesty said unto me, 'Thou hast come then! Thou hast smitten foreign lands and thou hast travelled, but now weakness hath vanquished thee, thou hast become old, and the infirmities of thy body are many. The warriors of the desert shall not escort thee [to thy grave] ... wilt thou not speak and declare thy name?' And I was afraid to contradict him, and I answered him about these matters like a man who was stricken with fear. Thus did my Lord speak to me.

And I answered and said, 'The matter was not of my doing, for, behold, it was done by the hand of God; bodily terror made me to flee according to what was ordained. But, behold, I am here in thy presence! Thou art life. Thy Majesty doeth as thou pleasest.' And the King dismissed the royal children, and His Majesty said unto the Queen, 'Look now, this is Sanehat who cometh in the guise of an Asiatic, and who hath turned himself into a nomad warrior of the desert.' And the Queen laughed a loud hearty laugh, and the royal children cried out with one voice before His Majesty, saying, 'O Lord King, this man cannot really be Sanehat'; and His Majesty said, 'It is indeed!'

Then the royal children brought their instruments of music, their menats and their sistra, and they rattled their sistra, and they passed backwards and forwards before His Majesty, saying, 'Thy hands perform beneficent acts, O King. The graces of the Lady of Heaven rest [upon thee]. The goddess Nubt giveth life to thy nostrils, and the Lady of the Stars joineth herself to thee, as thou sailest to the South wearing the Crown of the North, and to the North wearing the Crown of the South. Wisdom is stablished in the mouth of Thy Majesty, and health is on thy brow. Thou strikest terror into the miserable wretches who entreat thy mercy. Men propitiate thee, O Lord of Egypt, [as they do] Ra, and thou art acclaimed with cries of joy like Nebertcher. Thy horn conquereth, thine arrow slayeth, [but] thou givest breath to him that is afflicted. For our sakes graciously give a boon to this traveller Sanehat, this desert warrior who was born in Tamera (Egypt). He fled through fear of thee, and he departed to a far country because of his terror of thee. Doth not the face that gazeth on thine blench? Doth not the eye that gazeth into thine feel terrified?' Then His Majesty said, 'Let him fear not, and let him not utter a sound of fear. He shall be a smer official among the princes of the palace, he shall be a member of the company of the shenit officials. Get ye gone to the refectory of the palace, and see to it that rations are provided for him.'

Thereupon I came forth from the privy chamber of the King, and the royal children clasped my hands, and we passed on to the Great Door, and I was lodged in the house of one of the King's sons, which was beautifully furnished. In it there was a bath, and it contained representations of the heavens and objects from the Treasury. And there [I found] apparel made of royal linen, and myrrh of the finest quality which was used by the King, and every chamber was in charge of officials who were favourites of the King, and every officer had his own appointed duties. And [there] the years were made to slide off my members. I cut and combed my hair, I cast from me the dirt of a foreign land, together with the apparel of the nomads who live in the desert. I arrayed myself in apparel made of fine linen, I anointed my body with costly ointments, I slept upon a bedstead [instead of on the ground], I left the sand to those who dwelt on it, and the crude oil of wood wherewith they anoint themselves. I was allotted the house of a nobleman who had the title of smer, and many workmen laboured upon it, and its garden and its groves of trees were replanted with plants and trees. Rations were brought to me from the palace three or four times each day, in addition to the gifts which the royal children gave me unceasingly. And the site of a stone pyramid among the pyramids was marked out for me. The surveyor-in-chief to His Majesty chose the site for it, the director of the funerary designers drafted the designs and inscriptions which were to be cut upon it, the chief of the masons of the necropolis cut the inscriptions, and the clerk of the works in the necropolis went about the country collecting the necessary funerary furniture. I made the building to flourish, and provided everything that was necessary for its upkeep. I acquired land round about it. I made a lake for the performance of funerary ceremonies, and the land about it contained gardens, and groves of trees, and I provided a place where the people on the estate might dwell similar to that which is provided for a smeru nobleman of the first rank. My statue, which was made for me by

His Majesty, was plated with gold, and the tunic thereof was of silver-gold. Not for any ordinary person did he do such things. May I enjoy the favour of the King until the day of my death shall come!

Here endeth the book; [given] from its beginning to its end, as it hath been found in writing.

THE STORY OF THE EDUCATED PEASANT KHUENANPU

Translated by E. A. Wallis Budge

The text of this most interesting story is written in the hieratic character on papyri which are preserved in the British Museum and in the Royal Library at Berlin. It is generally thought that the story is the product of the period that immediately followed the XIIth Dynasty.

Once upon a time there lived a man whose name was Khuenanpu, a peasant of Sekhet-hemat, and he had a wife whose name was Nefert. This peasant said to this wife of his, 'Behold, I am going down into Egypt in order to bring back food for my children. Go thou and measure up the grain which remaineth in the granary, [and see how many] measures [there are].' Then she measured it, and there were eight measures. Then this peasant said unto this wife of his, 'Behold, two measures of grain shall be for the support of thyself and thy children, but of the other six thou shalt make bread and beer whereon I am to live during the days on which I shall be travelling.' And this peasant went down into Egypt, having laden his asses with *aaa* plants, and retmet plants, and soda and salt, and wood of the district of ..., and *aunt* wood of the Land of Oxen, and skins of panthers and wolves, and *neshau* plants, and *anu* stones, and *tenem* plants, and *kheperur* plants, and *sahut*, and *saksut* seeds (?), and *masut* plants, and *sent* and *abu* stones, and *absa* and *anba* plants, and doves and *naru* and *ukes* birds, and *tebu*, *uben* and *tebsu* plants, and *kenkent* seeds, and the plant 'hair of the earth', and *anset* seeds, and all kinds of beautiful products of the land of Sekhet-hemat. And when this peasant had marched to the south, to Hensu, and had arrived at the region of Perfefa, to the north of Metnat, he found a man standing on the river bank whose name was Tehutinekht, who was the son of a man whose name was Asri; both father and son were serfs of Rensi, the son of Meru the steward. When this man Tehutinekht saw the asses of this peasant, of which his heart approved greatly, he said, 'Would that I had any kind of god with me to help me to seize for myself the goods of this peasant!' Now the house of this Tehutinekht stood upon the upper edge of a sloping path along the river bank, which was narrow and not wide. It was about as wide as a sheet of linen cloth, and upon one side of it was the water of the stream, and on the other was a growing crop. Then this Tehutinekht said unto his slave, 'Run and bring me a sheet of linen out of my house'; and it was brought to him immediately. Then he shook out the sheet of linen over the narrow sloping path in such a way that its upper edge touched the water, and the fringed edge the growing crop. And when this peasant was going along the public path, this Tehutinekht said unto him, 'Be careful, peasant, wouldst thou walk upon my clothes?' And this peasant said, 'I will do as thou pleasest; my way is good.' And when he turned to the upper part of the path, this Tehutinekht said, 'Is my corn to serve as a road for thee, O peasant?' Then this peasant said, 'My way is good. The river-bank is steep, and the road is covered up with thy corn, and thou hast blocked up the path with thy linen garment. Dost thou really intend not to let us pass? Hath it come to pass that he dareth to say such a thing?' [At that moment] one of the asses bit off a large mouthful of the growing corn, and this Tehutinekht said, 'Behold, thy ass is eating my corn! Behold, he shall come and tread it out.' Then this peasant said, 'My way is good. Because one side of the road was made impassable [by thee], I led my ass to the other side (?), and now thou hast seized my ass because he bit off a large mouthful of the growing corn. However, I know the master of this estate, which belongeth to Rensi, the son of Meru. There is no doubt that he hath driven every robber out of the whole country, and shall I be robbed on his estate?' And this Tehutinekht said, 'Is not this an illustration of the proverb which the people use, "The name of the poor man is only mentioned because of his master?" It is I who speak to thee, but it is the steward [Rensi, the son of Meru] of whom thou art thinking.' Then Tehutinekht seized a cudgel of green tamarisk wood, and beat cruelly with it every part of the peasant's body, and took his asses from him and carried them off into his compound. And this peasant wept and uttered loud shrieks of pain because of what was done to him. And this Tehutinekht said, 'Howl not so loudly, peasant, or verily [thou shalt depart] to the domain of the Lord of Silence.' Then this peasant said, 'Thou hast beaten me, and robbed me of my possessions, and now thou wishest to steal even the very complaint that cometh out of my mouth! Lord of Silence indeed! Give me back my goods. Do not make me to utter complaints about thy fearsome character.'

And this peasant spent ten whole days in making entreaties to this Tehutinekht [for the restoration of his goods], but Tehutinekht paid no attention to them whatsoever. At the end of this time this peasant set out on a journey to the south, to the city of Hensu, in order to lay his complaint before Rensi, the son of Meru, the steward, and he found him just as he was coming forth from the door in the courtyard of his house which opened on the river bank, to embark in his official boat on the river. And this peasant said, 'I earnestly wish that it may happen that I may make glad thy heart with the words which I am going to say! Peradventure thou wilt allow some one to call thy confidential servant to me, in order that I may send him back to thee thoroughly well informed as to my business.' Then Rensi, the son of Meru, the steward, caused his confidential servant to go to this peasant, who sent him back to him thoroughly well informed as to his business. And Rensi, the son of Meru, the steward, made inquiries about this Tehutinekht from the officials who were immediately connected with him, and they said unto him, 'Lord, the matter is indeed only one that concerneth one of the peasants of Tehutinekht who went [to do business] with another man near him instead of with him. And, as a matter of fact, [officials like Tehutinekht] always treat their peasants in this manner whensoever they go to do business with other people instead of with them. Wouldst thou trouble thyself to inflict punishment upon Tehutinekht for the sake of a little soda and a little salt? [It is unthinkable.] Just let Tehutinekht be ordered to restore the soda and the salt and he will do so [immediately].' And Rensi, the son of Meru, the steward, held his peace; he made no answer to the words of these officials, and to this peasant he made no reply whatsoever.

And this peasant came to make his complaint to Rensi, the son of Meru, the steward, and on the first occasion he said, 'O my lord steward, greatest one of the great ones, guide of the things that are not and of these that are, when thou goest down into the Sea of Truth, and dost sail thereon, may the attachment (?) of thy sail not tear away, may thy boat not drift (?), may no accident befall thy mast, may the poles of thy boat not be broken, mayest thou not run aground when thou wouldst walk on the land, may the current not carry thee away, mayest thou not taste the calamities of the stream, mayest thou never see a face of fear, may the timid fish come to thee, and mayest thou obtain fine, fat waterfowl. O thou who art the father of the orphan, the husband of the widow, the brother of the woman who hath been put away by her husband, and the clother of the motherless, grant that I may place thy name in this land in connection with all good law. Guide in whom there is no avarice, great man in whom there is no meanness, who destroyest falsehood and makest what is true to exist, who comest to the word of my mouth, I speak that thou mayest hear. Perform justice, O thou who art praised, to whom those who are most worthy of praise give praise. Do away the oppression that weigheth me down. Behold, I am weighted with sorrow, behold, I am sorely wronged. Try me, for behold, I suffer greatly.'

Now this peasant spake these words in the time of the King of the South, the King of the North, NebkauRa, whose word is truth. And Rensi, the son of Meru, the steward, went into the presence of His Majesty, and said, 'My Lord, I have found one of these peasants who can really speak with true eloquence. His goods have been stolen from him by an official who is in my service, and behold, he hath come to lay before me a complaint concerning this.' His Majesty said unto Rensi, the son of Meru, the steward, 'If thou wouldst see me in a good state of health, keep him here, and do not make any answer at all to anything which he shall say, so that he may continue to speak. Then let that which he shall say be done into writing, and brought unto us, so that we may hear it. Take care that his wife and his children have food to live upon, and see that one of these peasants goeth to remove want from his house. Provide food for the peasant himself to live upon, but thou shalt make the provision in such a way that the food may be given to him without letting him know that it is thou who hast given it to him. Let the food be given to his friends and let them give it to him.' So there were given unto him four bread-cakes and two pots of beer daily. These were provided by Rensi, the son of

Meru, the steward, and he gave them to a friend, and it was this friend who gave them to the peasant. And Rensi, the son of Meru, the steward, sent instructions to the governor of [the Oasis of] Sekhet-hemat to supply the wife of the peasant with daily rations, and there were given unto her regularly the bread-cakes that were made from three measures of corn.

Then this peasant came a second time to lay his complaint [before Rensi], and he found him as he was coming out from the ..., and he said, 'O steward, my lord, the greatest of the great, thou richest of the rich, whose greatness is true greatness, whose riches are true riches, thou rudder of heaven, thou pole of the earth, thou measuring rope for heavy weights (?)! O rudder, slip not, O pole, topple not, O measuring rope, make no mistake in measuring! The great lord taketh away from her that hath no master (or owner), and stealeth from him that is alone [in the world]. Thy rations are in thy house — a pot of beer and three bread-cakes. What dost thou spend in satisfying those who depend upon thee? Shall he who must die die with his people? Wilt thou be a man of eternity (i.e. wilt thou live for ever?) Behold, are not these things evils, namely, the balance that leaneth side-ways, the pointer of the balance that doth not show the correct weight, and an upright and just man who departeth from his path of integrity? Observe! the truth goeth badly with thee, being driven out of her proper place, and the officials commit acts of injustice. He who ought to estimate a case correctly giveth a wrong decision. He who ought to keep himself from stealing committeth an act of robbery. He who should be strenuous to arrest the man who breaketh the word (i.e. Law) in its smallest point, is himself guilty of departing therefrom. He who should give breath stifleth him that could breathe. The land that ought to give repose driveth repose away. He who should divide in fairness hath become a robber. He who should blot out the oppressor giveth him the command to turn the town into a waste of water. He who should drive away evil himself committeth acts of injustice.'

Then Rensi, the son of Meru, the steward, said [to the peasant], 'Doth thy case appear in thy heart so serious that I must have my servant [Tchutinekht] seized on thy account?' This peasant said, 'He who measureth the heaps of corn filcheth from them for himself, and he who filleth [the measure] for others robbeth his neighbours. Since he who should carry out the behests of the Law giveth the order to rob, who is to repress crime? He who should do away with offences against the Law himself committeth them. He who should act with integrity behaveth crookedly. He who doeth acts of injustice is applauded. When wilt thou find thyself able to resist and to put down acts of injustice? [When] the ... cometh to his place of yesterday the command cometh: "Do a [good] deed in order that one may do a [good] deed [to thee]," that is to say, "Give thanks unto everyone for what he doeth." This is to drive back the bolt before it is shot, and to give a command to the man who is already overburdened with orders. Would that a moment of destruction might come, wherein thy vines should be laid low, and thy geese diminished, and thy waterfowl be made few in number! [Thus] it cometh that the man who ought to see clearly hath become blind, and he who ought to hear distinctly hath become

deaf, and he who ought to be a just guide hath become one who leadeth into error. Observe! thou art strong and powerful. Thine arm is able to do deeds of might, and [yet] thy heart is avaricious. Compassion hath removed itself from thee. The wretched man whom thou hast destroyed crieth aloud in his anguish. Thou art like unto the messenger of the god Henti (the Crocodile-god). Set not out [to do evil] for the Lady of the Plague (i.e. Sekhmet)....
As there is nothing between thee and her for a certain purpose, so there is nothing against thee and her. If thou wilt not do it [then] she will not show compassion. The beggar hath the powerful owner of possessions (or revenues) robbed, and the man who hath nothing hath the man who hath secreted [much] stolen goods. To steal anything at all from the beggar is an absolute crime on the part of the man who is not in want, and [if he doth this] shall his action not be inquired into? Thou art filled full with thy bread, and art drunken with thy beer, and thou art rich [beyond count]. When the face of the steersman is directed to what is in front of him, the boat falleth out of its course, and saileth whithersoever it pleaseth. When the King [remaineth] in his house, and when thou workest the rudder, acts of injustice take place round about thee, complaints are widespread, and the loss (?) is very serious. And one saith, "What is taking place?" Thou shouldst make thyself a place of refuge [for the needy]. Thy quay should be safe. But observe! Thy town is in commotion. Thy tongue is righteous, make no mistake [in judgment]. The abominable behaviour of a man is, as it were, [one of] his members. Speak no lies thyself, and take good heed that thy high officials do not do so. Those who

assess the dues on the crops are like unto a …, and to tell lies is very dear to their hearts. Thou who hast knowledge of the affairs of all the people, dost thou not understand my circumstances? Observe, thou who relievest the wants of all who have suffered by water, I am on the path of him that hath no boat. O thou who bringest every drowning man to land, and who savest the man whose boat hath foundered, art thou going to let me perish?'

And this peasant came a third time to lay his complaint [before Rensi], and he said, 'O my Lord Rensi, the steward! Thou art Ra, the lord of heaven with thy great chiefs. The affairs of all men [are ruled by thee]. Thou art like the water-flood. Thou art Hep (the Nile-god) who maketh green the fields, and who maketh the islands that are deserts to become productive. Exterminate the robber, be thou the advocate of those who are in misery, and be not towards the petitioner like the water-flood that sweepeth him away. Take heed to thyself likewise, for eternity cometh, and behave in such a way that the proverb, "Righteousness (or truth) is the breath of the nostrils," may be applicable unto thee. Punish those who are deserving of punishment, and then these shall be like unto thee in dispensing justice. Do not the small scales weigh incorrectly? Doth not the large balance incline to one side? In such cases is not Thoth merciful? When thou doest acts of injustice thou becomest the second of these three, and if these be merciful thou also mayest be merciful. Answer not good with evil, and do not set one thing in the place of another. Speech flourisheth more than the senmitplants, and groweth stronger than the smell of the same. Make no answer to it whilst thou pourest out acts of injustice, to make to grow apparel, which three ... will cause him to make. [If] thou workest the steering pole against the sail (?), the flood shall gather strength against the doing of what is right. Take good heed to thyself and set thyself on the mat (?) on the look-out place. The equilibrium of the earth is maintained by the doing of what is right. Tell not lies, for thou art a great man. Act not in a light manner, for thou art a man of solid worth. Tell not lies, for thou art a pair of scales. Make no mistake [in thy weighing], for thou art a correct reckoner (?). Observe! Thou art all of a piece with the pair of scales. If they weigh incorrectly, thou also shalt act falsely. Let not the boat run aground when thou art working the steering pole ... the look-out place. When thou hast to proceed against one who hath carried off something, take thou nothing, for behold, the great man ceaseth to be a great man when he is avaricious. Thy tongue is the pointer of the scales; thy heart is the weight; thy lips are the two arms of the scales. If thou coverest thy face so as not to see the doer of violent deeds, who is there [left] to repress lawless deeds? Observe! Thou art like a poor man for the man who washeth clothes, who is avaricious and destroyeth kindly feeling (?). He who forsaketh the friend who endoweth him for the sake of his client is his brother, who hath come and brought him a gift. Observe! Thou art a ferryman who ferriest over the stream only the man who possesseth the proper fare, whose integrity is well attested (?). Observe! Thou art like the overseer of a granary who doth not at once permit to pass him that cometh empty. Observe! Thou art among men like a bird of prey that liveth upon weak little birds. Observe! Thou art like the cook whose sole joy is to kill, whom no creature escapeth. Observe! Thou art like a shepherd who is careless about the loss of his sheep through the rapacious crocodile; thou never countest [thy sheep]. Would that thou wouldst make evil and rapacious men to be fewer! Safety hath departed from [every] town throughout the land. Thou shouldst hear, but most assuredly thou hearest not! Why hast thou not heard that I have this day driven back the rapacious man? When the crocodile pursueth.... How long is this condition of thine to last? Truth which is concealed shall be found, and falsehood shall perish. Do not imagine that thou art master of to-morrow, which hath not yet come, for the evils which it may bring with it are unknown.'

And behold, when this peasant had said these things to Rensi, the son of Meru, the steward, at the entrance to the hall of the palace, Rensi caused two men with leather whips to seize him, and they beat him in every member of his body. Then this peasant said: 'The son of Meru hath made a mistake. His face is blind in respect of what he seeth, he is deaf in respect of what he heareth, and he is forgetting that which he ought to remember. Observe! Thou art like unto a town that hath no governor, and a community that hath no chief, and a ship that hath no captain, and a body of men who have no guide. Observe! Thou art like a high official who is a thief, a governor of a town who taketh [bribes], and the overseer of a province who hath been appointed to suppress robbery, but who hath become the captain of those who practise it.'

And this peasant came a fourth time to lay his complaint before Rensi, and he met him as he was coming out from the door of the temple of the god Herushefit, and said, 'O thou who art praised, the god Herushefit, from whose house thou comest forth, praiseth thee. When well-doing perisheth, and there is none who seeketh to prevent its destruction, falsehood maketh itself seen boldly in the land. If it happen that the ferry-boat is not brought for thee to cross the stream in, how wilt thou be able to cross the stream? If thou hast to cross the stream in thy sandals, is thy crossing pleasant? Assuredly it is not! What man is there who continueth to sleep until it is broad daylight? [This habit] destroyeth the marching by night, and the travelling by day, and the possibility of a man profiting by his good luck, in very truth. Observe! One cannot tell thee sufficiently often that "Compassion hath departed from thee." And behold, how the oppressed man whom thou hast destroyed complaineth! Observe! Thou art like unto a man of the chase who would satisfy his craving for bold deeds, who determineth to do what he wisheth, to spear the hippopotamus, to shoot the wild bull, to catch fish, and to catch birds in his nets. He who is without hastiness will not speak without due thought. He whose habit is to ponder deeply will not be light-minded. Apply thy heart earnestly and thou shalt know the truth. Pursue diligently the course which thou hast chosen, and let him that heareth the plaintiff act rightly. He who followeth a right course of action will not treat a plaintiff wrongly. When the arm is brought, and when the two eyes see, and when the heart is of good courage, boast not loudly in proportion to thy strength, in order that calamity may not come unto thee. He who passeth by [his] fate halteth between two opinions. The man who eateth tasteth [his food], the man who is spoken to answereth, the man who sleepeth seeth visions, but nothing can resist the presiding judge when he is the pilot of the doer [of evil]. Observe, O stupid man, thou art apprehended. Observe, O ignorant man, thou art freely discussed. Observe, too, that men intrude upon thy most private moments. Steersman, let not thy boat run aground. Nourisher [of men], let not men die. Destroyer [of men], let not men perish. Shadow, let not men perish through the burning heat. Place of refuge, let not the crocodile commit ravages. It is now four times that I have laid my complaint before thee. How much more time shall I spend in doing this?'

This peasant came a fifth time to make his complaint, and said, 'O my lord steward, the fisherman with a khut instrument ..., the fisherman with a ... killeth i-fish, the fisherman with a harpoon speareth the āubbufish, the fisherman with a tchabhu instrument catcheth the paqru fish, and the common fishermen are always drawing fish from the river. Observe! Thou art even as they. Wrest not the goods of the poor man from him. The helpless man thou knowest him. The goods of the poor man are the breath of his life; to seize them and carry them off from him is to block up his nostrils. Thou art committed to the hearing of a case and to the judging between two parties at law, so that thou mayest suppress the robber; but, verily, what thou doest is to support the thief. The people love thee, and yet thou art a law-breaker. Thou hast been set as a dam before the man of misery, take heed that he is not drowned. Verily, thou art like a lake to him, O thou who flowest quickly.'

This peasant came the sixth time to lay his complaint [before Rensi], and said, 'O my lord steward ... who makest truth to be, who makest happiness (or, what is good) to be, who destroyest [all evil]; thou art like unto the satiety that cometh to put an end to hunger, thou art like unto the raiment that cometh to do away nakedness; thou art like unto the heavens that become calm after a violent storm and refresh with warmth those who are cold; thou art like unto the fire that cooketh that which is raw, and thou art like unto the water that quencheth the thirst. Yet look round about thee! He who ought to make a division fairly is a robber. He who ought to make everyone to be satisfied hath been the cause of the trouble. He who ought to be the source of healing is one of those who cause sicknesses. The transgressor diminisheth the truth. He who filleth well the right measure acteth rightly, provided that he giveth neither too little nor too much. If an offering be brought unto thee, do thou share it with thy brother (or neighbour), for that which is given in charity is free from after-thought (?). The man who is dissatisfied induceth separation, and the man who hath been condemned bringeth on schisms, even before one can know what is in his mind. When thou hast arrived at a decision delay not in declaring it. Who keepeth within him that which he can eject?... When a boat cometh into port it is unloaded, and the freight thereof is landed everywhere on the quay. It is [well] known that thou hast been educated, and trained, and experienced, but behold, it is not that thou mayest rob [the people]. Nevertheless thou dost [rob them] just as other people do, and those who are found about thee are thieves (?). Thou who shouldst be the most upright man of all the people art the greatest transgressor in the whole country. [Thou art] the wicked gardener who watereth his plot of ground with evil deeds in order to make his plot to tell lies, so that he may flood the town (or estate) with evil deeds (or calamities).'

This peasant came the seventh time in order to lay his complaint [before Rensi], and said, 'O my lord steward, thou art the steering pole of the whole land, and the land saileth according to thy command. Thou art the second (or counterpart) of Thoth, who judgeth impartially. My lord, permit thou a man to appeal to thee in respect of his cause which is righteous. Let not thy heart fight against it, for it is unseemly for thee to do so; [if thou doest this] thou of the broad face wilt become evil-hearted. Curse not the thing that hath not yet taken place, and rejoice not over that which hath not yet come to pass. The tolerant judge rejoiceth in showing kindness, and he withholdeth all action concerning a decision that hath been given, when he knoweth not what plan was in the heart. In the case of the judge who breaketh the Law, and overthroweth uprightness, the poor man cannot live [before him], for the judge plundereth him, and the truth saluteth him not. But my body is full, and my heart is overloaded, and the expression thereof cometh forth from my body by reason of the condition of the same. [When] there is a breach in the dam the water poureth out through it: even so is my mouth opened and it uttereth speech. I have now emptied myself, I have poured out what I had to pour out, I have unburdened my body, I have finished washing my linen. What I had to say before thee is said, my misery hath been fully set out before thee; now what hast thou to say in excuse (or apology)? Thy lazy cowardice hath been the cause of thy sin, thine avarice hath rendered thee stupid, and thy gluttony hath been thine enemy. Thinkest thou that thou wilt never find another peasant like unto me? If he hath a complaint to make thinkest thou that he will not stand, if he is a lazy man, at the door of his house? He whom thou forcest to speak will not remain silent. He whom thou forcest to wake up will not remain asleep. The faces which thou makest keen will not remain stupid. The mouth which thou openest will not remain closed. He whom thou makest intelligent will not remain ignorant. He whom thou instructest will not remain a fool. These are they who destroy evils. These are the officials, the lords of what is good. These are the crafts-folk who make what existeth. These are they who put on their bodies again the heads that have been cut off.'

This peasant came the eighth time to lay his complaint [before Rensi], and said, 'O my lord steward, a man falleth because of covetousness. The avaricious man hath no aim, for his aim is frustrated. Thy heart is avaricious, which befitteth thee not. Thou plunderest, and thy plunder is no use to thee. And yet formerly thou didst permit a man to enjoy that to which he had good right! Thy daily bread is in thy house, thy belly is filled, grain overfloweth [in thy granaries], and the overflow perisheth and is wasted. The officials who have been appointed to suppress acts of injustice have been rapacious robbers, and the officials who have been appointed to stamp out falsehood have become hiding-places for those who work iniquity. It is not fear of thee that hath driven me to make my complaint to thee, for thou dost not understand my mind (or heart). The man who is silent and who turneth back in order to bring his miserable state [before thee] is not afraid to place it before thee, and his brother doth not bring [gifts] from the interior of [his quarter]. Thy estates are in the fields, thy food is on [thy] territory, and thy bread is in the storehouse, yet the officials make gifts to thee and thou seizest them. Art thou not then a robber? Will not the men who plunder hasten with thee to the divisions of the fields? Perform the truth for the Lord of Truth, who possesseth the real truth. Thou writing reed, thou roll of papyrus, thou palette, thou Thoth, thou art remote from acts of justice. O Good One, thou art still goodness. O Good One, thou art truly good. Truth endureth for ever. It goeth down to the grave with those who perform truth, it is laid in the coffin and is buried in the earth; its name is never removed from the earth, and its name is remembered on earth for good (or blessing). That is the ordinance of the word of God. If it be a matter of a hand-balance it never goeth askew; if it be a matter of a large pair of scales, the standard thereof never inclineth to one side. Whether it be I who come, or another, verily thou must make speech, but do not answer whether thou speakest to one who ought to hold his peace, or whether thou seizest one who cannot seize thee. Thou art not merciful, thou art not considerate. Thou hast not withdrawn thyself, thou hast not gone afar off. But thou hast not in any way given in respect of me any judgment in accordance with the command, which came forth from the mouth of Ra himself, saying, "Speak the truth, perform the truth, for truth is great, mighty, and everlasting. When thou performest the truth thou wilt find its virtues (?), and it will lead thee to the state of being blessed (?). If the hand-balance is askew, the pans of the balance, which perform the weighing, hang crookedly, and a correct weighing cannot be carried out, and the result is a false one; even so the result of wickedness is wickedness.'"

This peasant came the ninth time to lay his complaint [before Rensi], and said, 'The great balance of men is their tongues, and all the rest is put to the test by the hand balance. When thou punishest the man who ought to be punished, the act telleth in thy favour. [When he doeth not this] falsehood becometh his possession, truth turneth away from before him, his goods are falsehood, truth forsaketh him, and supporteth him not. If falsehood advanceth, she maketh a mistake, and goeth not over with the ferry-boat [to the Island of Osiris]. The man with whom falsehood prevaileth hath no children and no heirs upon the earth. The man in whose boat falsehood saileth never reacheth land, and his boat never cometh into port. Be not heavy, but at the same time do not be too light. Be not slow, but at the same time be not too quick. Rage not at the man who is listening to thee. Cover not over thy face before the man with whom thou art acquainted. Make not blind thy face towards the man who is looking at thee. Thrust not aside the suppliant as thou goest down. Be not indolent in making known thy decision. Do [good] unto him that will do [good] unto thee. Hearken not unto the cry of the mob, who say, "A man will assuredly cry out when his case is really righteous." There is no yesterday for the indolent man, there is no friend for the man who is deaf to [the words of] truth, and there is no day of rejoicing for the avaricious man. The informer becometh a poor man, and the poor man becometh a beggar, and the unfriendly man becometh a dead person. Observe now, I have laid my complaint before thee, but thou wilt not hearken unto it; I shall now depart, and make my complaint against thee to Anubis.'

Then Rensi, the son of Meru, the steward, caused two of his servants to go and bring back the peasant. Now this peasant was afraid, for he believed that he would be beaten severely because of the words which he had spoken to him. And this peasant said, 'This is [like] the coming of the thirsty man to salt tears, and the taking of the mouth of the suckling child to the breast of the woman that is dry. That the sight of which is longed for cometh not, and only death approacheth.'

Then Rensi, the son of Meru, the steward, said, 'Be not afraid, O peasant, for behold, thou shalt dwell with me.' Then this peasant swore an oath, saying, 'Assuredly I will eat of thy bread, and drink of thy beer for ever.' Then Rensi, the son of Meru, the steward, said, 'Come hither, however, so that thou mayest hear thy petitions'; and he caused to be [written] on a roll of new papyrus all the complaints which this peasant had made, each complaint according to its day. And Rensi, the son of Meru, the steward, sent the papyrus to the King of the South, the King of the North, NebkauRa, whose word is truth, and it pleased the heart of His Majesty more than anything else in the whole land. And His Majesty said, 'Pass judgment on thyself, O son of Meru.' And Rensi, the son of Meru, the steward, despatched two men to bring him back. And he was brought back, and an embassy was despatched to Sekhet-hemat.... Six persons, besides ... his grain, and his millet, and his asses, and his dogs.... [The remaining lines are mutilated, but the words which are visible make it certain that Tehutinekht the thief was punished, and that he was made to restore to the peasant everything which he had stolen from him.]

THE JOURNEY OF THE PRIEST UNU-AMEN INTO SYRIA TO BUY CEDAR WOOD TO MAKE A NEW BOAT FOR AMEN-RA

Translated by E. A. Wallis Budge

The text of this narrative is written in the hieratic character upon a papyrus preserved in St Petersburg; it gives an excellent description of the troubles that befell the priest Unu-Amen during his journey into Syria in the second half of the eleventh century BC.

On the eighteenth day of the third month of the season of the Inundation, of the fifth year, Unu-Amen, the senior priest of the Hait chamber of the house of Amen, the Lord of the thrones of the Two Lands, set out on his journey to bring back wood for the great and holy Boat of Amen-Ra, the King of the Gods, which is called 'User-hat', and floateth on the canal of Amen. On the day wherein I arrived at Tchān (Tanis or Zoan), the territory of Nessubanebtet (i.e. King Smendes) and Thent-Amen, I delivered unto them the credentials which I had received from Amen-Ra, the King of the Gods, and when they had had my letters read before them, they said, 'We will certainly do whatsoever Amen-Ra, the King of the Gods, our Lord, commandeth.' And I lived in that place until the fourth month of the season of the Inundation, and I abode in the palace at Zoan. Then Nessubanebtet and Thent-Amen despatched me with the captain of the large ship called *Menkabuta*, and I set sail on the sea of Kharu (Syria) on the first day of the fourth month of the Season of the Inundation. I arrived at Dhir, a city of Tchakaru, and Badhilu, its prince, made his servants bring me bread-cakes by the ten thousand, and a large jar of wine, and a leg of beef. And a man who belonged to the crew of my boat ran away, having stolen vessels of gold that weighed five teben, and four vessels of silver that weighed twenty teben, and silver in a leather bag that weighed eleven teben; thus he stole five teben of gold and thirty-one teben of silver.

On the following morning I rose up, and I went to the place where the prince of the country was, and I said unto him, 'I have been robbed in thy port. Since thou art the prince of this land, and the leader thereof, thou must make search and find out what hath become of my money. I swear unto thee that the money [once] belonged to Amen-Ra, King of the Gods, the Lord of the Two

Lands; it belonged to Nessubanebtet, it belonged to my lord Her-Heru, and to the other great kings of Egypt, but it now belongeth to Uartha, and to Makamāru, and to Tchakar-Bāl, Prince of Kepuna (Byblos).' And he said unto me, 'Be angry or be pleased, [as thou likest], but, behold, I know absolutely nothing about the matter of which thou speakest unto me. Had the thief been a man who was a subject of mine, who had gone down into thy ship and stolen thy money, I would in that case have made good thy loss from the moneys in my own treasury, until such time as it had been found out who it was that robbed thee, and what his name was, but the thief who hath robbed thee belongeth to thine own ship. Yet tarry here for a few days, and stay with me, so that I may seek him out.' So I tarried there for nine days, and my ship lay at anchor in his port. And I went to him and I said unto him, 'Verily thou hast not found my money, [but I must depart] with the captain of the ship and with those who are travelling with him.' ... [The text here is mutilated, but from the fragments of the lines that remain it seems clear that Unu-Amen left the port of Dhir, and proceeded in his ship to Tyre. After a short stay there he left Tyre very early one morning and sailed to Kepuna (Byblos), so that he might have an interview with the governor of that town, who was called Tchakar-Bāl. During his interview with Tchakar-Bāl the governor of Tyre produced a bag containing thirty teben of silver, and Unu-Amen promptly seized it, and declared that he intended to keep it until his own money which had been stolen was returned to him. Whilst Unu-Amen was at Byblos he buried in some secret place the image of the god Amen and the amulets belonging to it, which he had brought with him to protect him and to guide him on his way. The name of this image was 'Amenta-mat.' The text then proceeds in a connected form thus:]

And I passed nineteen days in the port of Byblos, and the governor passed his days in sending messages to me each day, saying, 'Get thee gone out of my harbour.' Now on one occasion when he was making an offering to his gods, the god took possession of a certain young chief of his chiefs, and he caused him to fall into a fit of frenzy, and the young man said, 'Bring up the god. Bring the messenger who hath possession of him. Make him to set out on his way. Make him to depart immediately.' Now the man who had been seized with the fit of divine frenzy continued to be moved by the same during the night. And I found a certain ship, which was bound for Egypt, and when I had transferred to it all my property, I cast a glance at the darkness, saying, 'If the darkness increaseth I will transfer the god to the ship also, and not permit any other eye whatsoever to look upon him.' Then the superintendent of the harbour came unto me, saying, 'Tarry thou here until to-morrow morning, according to the orders of the governor.' And I said unto him, 'Art not thou thyself he who hath passed his days in coming to me daily and saying, "Get thee gone out of my harbour?" Dost thou not say, "Tarry here," so that I may let the ship which I have found [bound for Egypt] depart, when thou wilt again come and say, "Haste thee to be gone"?'

And the superintendent of the harbour turned away and departed, and told the governor what I had said. And the governor sent a message to the captain of the ship bound for Egypt, saying,

'Tarry till the morning; these are the orders of the governor.' And when the morning had come, the governor sent a messenger, who took me to the place where offerings were being made to the god in the fortress wherein the governor lived on the sea coast. And I found him seated in his upper chamber, and he was reclining with his back towards an opening in the wall, and the waves of the great Syrian sea were rolling in from seawards and breaking on the shore behind him. And I said unto him, 'The grace of Amen [be with thee]!' And he said unto me, 'Including this day, how long is it since thou camest from the place where Amen is?' And I said unto him, 'Five months and one day, including to-day.' And he said unto me, 'Verily if that which thou sayest is true, where are the letters of Amen which ought to be in thy hand? Where are the letters of the high priest of Amen which ought to be in thy hand?'

And I said unto him, 'I gave them to Nessubanebtet and Thent-Amen.' Then was he very angry indeed, and he said unto me, 'Verily, there are neither letters nor writings in thy hands for us! Where is the ship made of acacia wood which Nessubanebtet gave unto thee? Where are his Syrian sailors? Did he not hand thee over to the captain of the ship so that after thou hadst started on thy journey they might kill thee and cast thee into the sea? Whose permission did they seek to attack the god? And indeed whose permission were they seeking before they attacked thee?' This is what he said unto me.

And I said unto him, 'The ship [wherein I sailed] was in very truth an Egyptian ship, and it had a crew of Egyptian sailors who sailed it on behalf of Nessubanebtet. There were no Syrian sailors placed on board of it by him.' He said unto me, 'I swear that there are twenty ships lying in my harbour, the captains of which are in partnership with Nessubanebtet. And as for the city of Sidon, whereto thou wishest to travel, I swear that there are there ten thousand other ships, the captains of which are in partnership with Uarkathar, and they are sailed for the benefit of his house.' At this grave moment I held my peace. And he answered and said unto me, 'On what matter of business hast thou come hither?' And I said unto him, 'The matter concerning which I have come is wood for the great and holy Boat of Amen-Ra, the King of the Gods. What thy father did [for the god], and what thy father's father did for him, do thou also.' That was what I said unto him. And he said unto me, 'They certainly did do work for it (i.e. the boat). Give me a gift for my work for the boat, and then I also will work for it. Assuredly my father and my grandfather did do the work that was demanded of them, and Pharaoh, life, strength, and health be to him! caused six ships laden with the products of Egypt to come hither, and the contents thereof were unloaded into their storehouses. Now, thou must most certainly cause some goods to be brought and given to me for myself.'

Then he caused to be brought the books which his father had kept day by day, and he had them read out before me, and it was found that one thousand teben of silver of all kinds were [entered] in his books. And he said unto me, 'If the Ruler of Egypt had been the lord of my possessions, and if I had indeed been his servant, he would never have had silver and gold brought [to pay my father and my father's father] when he told them to carry out the commands of Amen. The instructions which they (i.e. Pharaoh) gave to my father were by no means the command of one who was their king. As for me, I am assuredly not thy servant, and indeed I am not the servant of him that made thee to set out on thy way. If I were to cry out now, and to shout to the cedars of Lebanon, the heavens would open, and the trees would be lying spread out on the sea-shore. I ask thee now to show me the sails which thou hast brought to carry thy ships which shall be loaded with thy timber to Egypt. And show me also the tackle with which thou wilt transfer to thy ships the trees which I shall cut down for thee for.... [Unless I make for thee the tackle] and the sails of thy ships, the tops will be too heavy, and they will snap off, and thou wilt perish in the midst of the sea, [especially if] Amen uttereth his voice in the sky, and he unfettereth Sutekh at the moment when he rageth. Now Amen hath assumed the overlordship of all lands, and he hath made himself their master, but first and foremost he is the overlord of Egypt, whence thou hast come. Excellent things have come forth from Egypt, and have reached even unto this place wherein I am; and moreover, knowledge (or learning) hath come forth therefrom, and hath reached even unto this place wherein I am. But of what use is this beggarly journey of thine which thou hast been made to take?'

And I said unto him, 'What a shameful thing [to say]! It is not a beggarly journey whereon I have been despatched by those among whom I live. And besides, assuredly there is not a single boat that floateth that doth not belong to Amen. To him belong the sea and the cedars of Lebanon, concerning which thou sayest,

"They are my property." In Lebanon groweth [the wood] for the Boat Amen-userhat, the lord of boats. Amen-Ra, the King of the Gods, spake and told Her-Heru, my lord, to send me forth; and therefore he caused me to set out on my journey together with this great god. Now behold, thou hast caused this great god to pass nine and twenty days here in a boat that is lying at anchor in thy harbour, for most assuredly thou didst know that he was resting here. Amen is now what he hath always been, and yet thou wouldst dare to stand up and haggle about the [cedars of] Lebanon with the god who is their lord! And as concerning what thou hast spoken, saying, "The kings of Egypt in former times caused silver and gold to be brought [to my father and father's father, thou art mistaken]." Since they had bestowed upon them life and health, they would never have caused gold and silver to be brought to them; but they might have caused gold and silver to be brought to thy fathers instead of life and health. And Amen-Ra, the King of the Gods, is the Lord of life and health. He was the god of thy fathers, and they served him all their lives, and made offerings unto him, and indeed thou thyself art a servant of Amen. If now thou wilt say unto Amen, "I will perform thy commands, I will perform thy commands," and wilt bring this business to a prosperous ending, thou shalt live, thou shalt be strong, thou shalt be healthy, and thou shalt rule thy country to its uttermost limits wisely and well, and thou shalt do good to thy people. But take good heed that thou lovest not the possessions of Amen-Ra, the King of the Gods, for the lion loveth the things that belong unto him. And now, I pray thee to allow my scribe to be summoned to me, and I will send him to Nessubanebtet and Thent-Amen, the local governors whom Amen hath appointed to rule the northern portion of his land, and they will send to me everything which I shall tell them to send to me, saying, "Let such and such a thing be brought," until such time as I can make the journey to the South (i.e. to Egypt), when I will have thy miserable dross brought to thee, even to the uttermost portion thereof, in very truth.' That was what I said unto him.

And he gave my letter into the hand of his ambassador. And he loaded up on a ship wood for the fore part and wood for the hind part [of the Boat of Amen], and four other trunks of cedar trees which had been cut down, in all seven trunks, and he despatched them to Egypt. And his ambassador departed to Egypt, and he returned to me in Syria in the first month of the winter season (November–December). And Nessubanebtet and Thent-Amen sent to me five vessels of gold, five vessels of silver, ten pieces of byssus, each sufficiently large to make a suit of raiment, five hundred rolls of fine papyrus, five hundred hides of oxen, five hundred ropes, twenty sacks of lentils, and thirty vessels full of dried fish. And for my personal use they sent to me five pieces of byssus, each sufficiently large to make a suit of raiment, a sack of lentils, and five vessels full of dried fish. Then the Governor was exceedingly glad and rejoiced greatly, and he sent three hundred men and three hundred oxen [to Lebanon] to cut down the cedar trees, and he appointed overseers to direct them. And they cut down the trees, the trunks of which lay there during the whole of the winter season. And when the third month of the summer season had come, they dragged the tree trunks down to the sea-shore. And the Governor came out of his palace, and took up his stand before the trunks, and he sent a message to me, saying, 'Come.' Now as I was passing close by him, the shadow of his umbrella fell upon me, whereupon Pen-Amen, an officer of his bodyguard, placed himself between him and me, saying, 'The shadow of Pharaoh, life, strength, and health, be to him! thy Lord, falleth upon thee.' And the Governor was wroth with Pen-Amen, and he said, 'Let him alone.' Therefore I walked close to him.

And the Governor answered and said unto me, 'Behold, the orders [of Pharaoh] which my fathers carried out in times of old, I also have carried out, notwithstanding the fact that thou hast not done for me what thy fathers were wont to do for me. However, look for thyself, and take note that the last of the cedar trunks hath arrived, and here it lieth. Do now whatsoever thou pleaseth with them, and take steps to load them into ships, for assuredly they are given to thee as a gift. I beg thee to pay no heed to the terror of the sea voyage, but if thou persistest in contemplating [with fear] the sea voyage, thou must also contemplate [with fear] the terror of me [if thou tarriest here]. Certainly I have not treated thee as the envoys of Khā-em-Uast were treated here, for they were made to pass seventeen (or fifteen) years in this country, and they died here.'

Then the Governor spake to the officer of his bodyguard, saying, 'Lay hands on him, and take him to see the tombs wherein they lie.' And I said unto him, 'Far be it from me to look upon such [ill-omened] things! As concerning the messengers of Khā-em-Uast, the men whom he sent unto thee as ambassadors were merely [officials] of his, and there was no god with his ambassadors, and so thou sayest, "Make haste to look upon thy colleagues." Behold, wouldst thou not have greater pleasure, and shouldst thou not [instead of saying such things] cause to be made a stele whereon should be said by thee:

'Amen-Ra, the King of the Gods, sent to me Amen-ta-mat, his divine ambassador, together with Unu-Amen, his human ambassador, in quest of trunks of cedar wood for the Great and Holy Boat of Amen-Ra, the King of the Gods. And I cut down cedar trees, and I loaded them into ships. I provided the ships myself, and I manned them with my own sailors, and I made them to arrive in Egypt that they might bespeak [from the god for me] ten thousand years of life, in addition to the span of life which was decreed for me. And this petition hath been granted.

'[And wouldst thou not rather] that, after the lapse of time, when another ambassador came from the land of Egypt who understood this writing, he should utter thy name which should be on the stele, and pray that thou shouldst receive water in Amentet, even like the gods who subsist?'

And he said unto me, 'These words which thou hast spoken unto me are of a certainty a great testimony.' And I said unto him, 'Now, as concerning the multitude of words which thou hast spoken unto me: As soon as I arrive at the place where the First Prophet (i.e. Her-Heru) of Amen dwelleth, and he knoweth [how thou hast] performed the commands of the God [Amen], he will cause to be conveyed to thee [a gift of] certain things.' Then I walked down to the beach, to the place where the trunks of cedar had been lying, and I saw eleven ships [ready] to put out to sea; and they belonged to Tchakar-Bāl. [And the governor sent out an order] saying, 'Stop him, and do not let any ship with him on board [depart] to the land of Egypt.' Then I sat myself down and wept. And the scribe of the Governor came out to me, and said unto me, 'What aileth thee?' And I said unto him, 'Consider the kashu birds that fly to Egypt again and again! And consider how they flock to the cool water brooks! Until the coming of whom must I remain cast aside hither? Assuredly thou seest those who have come to prevent my departure a second time.'

Then [the scribe] went away and told the Governor what I had said; and the Governor shed tears because of the words that had been repeated to him, for they were full of pain. And he caused the scribe to come out to me again, and he brought with him two skins [full] of wine and a goat. And he caused to be brought out to me Thentmut, an Egyptian singing woman who lived in his house, and he said to her, 'Sing to him, and let not the cares of his business lay hold upon his heart.' And to me he sent a message, saying, 'Eat and drink, and let not business lay hold upon thy heart. Thou shalt hear everything which I have to say unto thee to-morrow morning.'

And when the morning had come, he caused [the inhabitants of the town] to be assembled on the quay, and having stood up in their midst, he said to the Tchakaru, 'For what purpose have ye come hither?' And they said unto him, 'We have come hither seeking for the ships which have been broken and dashed to pieces, that is to say, the ships which thou didst despatch to Egypt, with our unfortunate fellow-sailors in them.' And he said unto them, 'I know not how to detain the ambassador of Amen in my country any longer. I beg of you to let me send him away, and then do ye pursue him, and prevent him [from escaping].' And he made me embark in a ship, and sent me forth from the sea-coast, and the winds drove me ashore to the land of Alasu (Cyprus?). And the people of the city came forth to slay me, and I was dragged along in their midst to the place where their queen Hathaba lived; and I met her when she was coming forth from one house to go into another. Then I cried out in entreaty to her, and I said unto the people who were standing about her, 'Surely there must be among you someone who understandeth the language of Egypt.' And one of them said, 'I understand the speech [of Egypt].' Then I said unto him, 'Tell my Lady these words: I have heard it said far from here, even in the city of [Thebes], the place where Amen dwelleth, that wrong is done in every city, and that only in the land of Alasu (Cyprus?) is right done. And yet wrong is done here every day!' And she said, 'What is it that thou really wishest to say?' I said unto her, 'Now that the angry sea and the winds have cast me up on the land wherein thou dwellest, thou wilt surely not permit these men who have received me to slay me! Moreover, I am an ambassador of Amen. And consider carefully, for I am a man who will be searched for every day. And as for the sailors of Byblos whom they wish to kill, if their lord findeth ten of thy sailors he will assuredly slay them.' Then she caused her people to be called off me, and they were made to stand still, and she said unto me, 'Lie down and sleep....' [The rest of the narrative is wanting.]

TALES OF THE MAGICIANS

Translated by E. A. Wallis Budge

The short stories of the wonderful deeds of ancient Egyptian magicians here given are found in the Westcar Papyrus. It was written probably at some period between the XIIth and XVIIIth Dynasties.

THE MAGICIAN UBAANER AND THE WAX CROCODILE

The first story describes an event which happened in the reign of Nebka, a king of the IIIrd Dynasty. It was told by Prince KhāfRa to King Khufu (Cheops). The magician was called Ubaaner, and he was the chief Kher-heb in the temple of Ptah of Memphis, and a very learned man. He was a married man, but his wife loved a young man who worked in the fields, and she sent him by the hands of one of her maids a box containing a supply of very fine clothes. Soon after receiving this gift the young man proposed to the magician's wife that they should meet and talk in a certain booth or lodge in her garden, and she instructed the steward to have the lodge made ready for her to receive her friend in it. When this was done, she went to the lodge, and she sat there with the young man and drank beer with him until the evening, when he went on his way. The steward, knowing what had happened, made up his mind to report the matter to his master, and as soon as the morning had come, he went to Ubaaner and informed him that his wife had spent the previous day drinking beer with such and such a young man. Ubaaner then told the steward to fetch him his casket made of ebony and silver-gold, which contained materials and instruments used in working magic, and when it was brought him, he took out some wax, and fashioned a figure of a crocodile seven spans long. He then recited certain magical words over the crocodile, and said to it, 'When the young man comes to bathe in my lake thou shalt seize him.' Then giving the wax crocodile to the steward, Ubaaner said to him, 'When the young man goes down to the lake to bathe according to his daily habit, thou shalt throw the crocodile into the water after him.' Having taken the crocodile from his master the steward departed.

Then the wife of Ubaaner told the steward to set the little lodge in the garden in order, because she was going to spend some time there. When the steward had furnished the lodge, she went there, and the young peasant paid her a visit. After leaving the lodge he went and bathed in the lake, and the steward followed him and threw the wax crocodile into the water; it immediately turned into a large crocodile 7 cubits (about 11 feet) long and seized the young man and swallowed him up. When this took place the magician Ubaaner was with the king, and he remained in attendance upon him for seven days, during which time the young man was in the lake, with no air to breathe. When the seven days were ended King Nebka proposed to take a walk with the magician. Whilst they were going along Ubaaner asked the king if he would care to see a wonderful thing that had happened to a young peasant, and the king said he would, and forthwith walked to the place to which the magician led him. When they arrived at the lake Ubaaner uttered a spell over the crocodile, and commanded it to come up out of the water bringing the young man with him; and the crocodile did so. When the king saw the beast he exclaimed at its hideousness, and seemed to be afraid of it, but the magician stooped down fearlessly, and took the crocodile up in his hand, and lo, the living crocodile had disappeared, and only a crocodile of wax remained in its place. Then Ubaaner told King Nebka the story of how the young man had spent days in the lodge in the garden talking and drinking beer with his wife, and His Majesty said to the wax crocodile, 'Get thee gone, and take what is thine with thee.' And the wax crocodile leaped out of the magician's hand into the lake, and once more became a large, living crocodile. And it swam away with the young man, and no one ever knew what became of it afterwards. Then the king made his servants seize Ubaaner's wife, and they carried her off to the ground on the north side of the royal palace, and there they burned her, and they scattered her ashes in the river. When King Khufu had heard the story he ordered many offerings to be made in the tomb of his predecessor Nebka, and gifts to be presented to the magician Ubaaner.

THE MAGICIAN TCHATCHAMĀNKH AND THE GOLD ORNAMENT

The Prince BaiufRa stood up and offered to relate to King Khufu (Cheops) a story of a magician called Tchatchamānkh, who flourished in the reign of Seneferu, the king's father. The offer having been accepted, BaiufRa proceeded to relate the following: On one occasion it happened that Seneferu was in a perplexed and gloomy state of mind, and he wandered distractedly about the rooms and courts of his palace seeking to find something wherewith to amuse himself, but he failed to do so. Then he bethought himself of the court magician Tchatchamānkh, and he ordered his servants to summon him to the presence. When the great Kher-heb and scribe arrived, he addressed him as 'my brother', and told him that he had been wandering about in his palace seeking for amusement, and had failed to find it. The magician promptly suggested to the king that he should have a boat got ready, decorated with pretty things that would give pleasure, and should go for a row on the lake. The motions of the rowers as they rowed the boat about would interest him, and the sight of the depths of the waters, and the pretty fields and gardens round about the lake, would give him great pleasure. 'Let me,' said the magician, 'arrange the matter. Give me twenty ebony paddles inlaid with gold and silver, and twenty pretty maidens with flowing hair, and twenty network garments wherein to dress them.' The king gave orders for all these things to be provided, and when the boat was ready, and the maidens who were to row had taken their places, he entered the boat and sat in his little pavilion and was rowed about on the lake. The magician's views proved to be correct, for the king enjoyed himself, and was greatly amused in watching the maidens row. Presently the handle of the paddle of one of the maidens caught in her long hair, and in trying to free it a malachite ornament which she was wearing in her hair fell into the water and disappeared. The maiden was much troubled over her loss, and stopped rowing, and as her stopping threw out of order the strokes of the maidens who were sitting on the same seat as she was, they also stopped rowing. Thereupon the king asked why the rowing had ceased, and one of the maidens told him what had happened; and when he promised that the ornament should be recovered, the maiden said words which seem to mean that she had no doubt that she should recover it. On this Seneferu caused Tchatchamānkh to be summoned into the presence, and when he came the king told him all that had happened. Then the magician began to recite certain spells, the effect of which was to cause the water of the lake first to divide into two parts, and then the water on one side to rise up and place itself on the water on the other side. The boat, presumably, sank down gently on the ground of the lake, for the malachite ornament was seen lying there, and the magician fetched it, and returned it to its owner. The depth of the water in the middle of the lake where the ornament dropped was 12 cubits (between 18 and 19 feet), and when the water from one side was piled up on that on the other, the total depth of the two sections taken together was, we are told, 24 cubits. As soon as the ornament was restored to the maiden, the magician recited further spells, and the water lowered itself, and spread over the ground of the lake, and so regained its normal level. His Majesty, King Seneferu, assembled his nobles, and having discussed the matter with them, made a handsome gift to his clever magician. When King Khufu had heard the story he ordered a large supply of funerary offerings to be sent to the tomb of Seneferu, and bread, beer, flesh, and incense to the tomb of Tchatchamānkh.

THE MAGICIAN TETA WHO RESTORED LIFE TO DEAD ANIMALS

When BaiufRa had finished the story given above, Prince Herutataf, the son of King Khufu, and a very wise man, with whose name Egyptian tradition associated the discovery of certain chapters of the Book of the Dead, stood up before his father to speak, and said to him, 'Up to the present thou hast only heard tales about the wisdom of magicians who are dead and gone, concerning which it is quite impossible to know whether they be true or not. Now, I want Thy Majesty to see a certain sage who is actually alive during thy lifetime, whom thou knowest not.' His Majesty Khufu said, 'Who is it, Herutataf?' And Prince Herutataf replied, 'He is a certain peasant who is called Teta, and he lives in Tet-Seneferu. He is one hundred and ten years old, and up to this very day he eats five hundred bread-cakes (sic), and a leg of beef, and drinks one hundred pots of beer. He knows how to reunite to its body a head which has been cut off, he knows how to make a lion follow him whilst the rope with which he is tied drags behind him on the ground, and he knows the numbers of the Apet chambers (?) of the shrine (?) of Thoth.' Now His Majesty had been seeking for a long time past for the number of the Apet chambers (?) of Thoth, for he had wished to make something like it for his 'horizon'. And King Khufu said to his son Herutataf, 'My son, thou thyself shalt go and bring the sage to me'; thereupon a boat was made ready for Prince Herutataf, who forthwith set out on his journey to Tet-Seneferu, the home of the sage. When the prince came to the spot on the river bank that was nearest to the village of Teta, he had the boat tied up, and he continued his journey overland seated in a sort of sedan chair made of ebony, which was carried or slung on bearing poles made of costly sesentchem wood inlaid or decorated with gold. When Herutataf arrived at the village, the chair was set down on the ground, and he got out of it and stood up ready to greet the old man, whom he found lying upon a bed, with the door of his house lying on the ground. One servant stood by the bed holding the sage's head and fanning him, and another was engaged in rubbing his feet. Herutataf addressed a highly poetical speech to Teta, the gist of which was that the old man seemed to be able to defy the usual effects of old age, and to be like one who had obtained the secret of everlasting youth, and then expressed the hope that he was well. Having paid these compliments, which were couched in dignified and archaic language, Herutataf went on to say that he had come with a message from his father Khufu, who hereby summoned Teta to his presence. 'I have come,' he said, 'a long way to invite thee, so that thou mayest eat the food, and enjoy the good things which the king bestows on those who follow him, and so that he may conduct thee after a happy life to thy fathers who rest in the grave.' The sage replied, 'Welcome, Prince Herutataf, welcome, O thou who lovest thy father. Thy father shall reward thee with gifts, and he shall promote thee to the rank of the senior officials of his court. Thy Ka shall fight successfully against thine enemy, thy soul knows the ways of the Other World, and thou shalt arrive at the door of those who are apparelled in ... I salute thee, O Prince Herutataf.'

Herutataf then held out his hands to the sage and helped him to rise from the bed, and he went with him to the river bank, Teta leaning on his arm. When they arrived there Teta asked for a boat wherein his children and his books might be placed, and the prince put at his disposal two boats, with crews complete; Teta himself, however, was accommodated in the prince's boat and sailed with him. When they came to the palace, Prince Herutataf went into the presence of the king to announce their arrival, and said to him, 'O king my lord, I have brought Teta'; and His Majesty replied, 'Bring him in quickly.' Then the king went out into the large hall of his palace, and Teta was led into the presence. His Majesty said,

'How is it, Teta, that I have never seen thee?' And Teta answered, 'Only the man who is summoned to the presence comes; so soon as the king summoned me I came.' His Majesty asked him, saying, 'Is it indeed true, as is asserted, that thou knowest how to rejoin to its body the head which hath been cut off?' Teta answered, 'Most assuredly do I know how to do this, O king my lord.' His Majesty said, 'Let them bring in from the prison a prisoner, so that his death-sentence may be carried out.' Then Teta said, 'Let them not bring a man, O king my lord. Perhaps it may be ordered that the head shall be cut off some other living creature.' So a goose was brought to him, and he cut off its head, and laid the body of the goose on the west side of the hall, and its head on the east side. Then Teta recited certain magical spells, and the goose stood up and waddled towards its head, and its head moved towards its body. When the body and the head came close together, the head leaped on to the body, and the goose stood up on its legs and cackled.

Then a goose of another kind called khetâa was brought to Teta, and he did with it as he had done with the other goose. His Majesty next caused an ox to be taken to Teta, and when he had cut off its head, and recited magical spells over the head and the body, the head rejoined itself to the body, and the ox stood up on its feet. A lion was next brought to Teta, and when he had recited spells over it, the lion went behind him, and followed him [like a dog], and the rope with which he had been tied up trailed on the ground behind the animal.

King Khufu then said to Teta, 'Is it true what they say that thou knowest the numbers of the Apet chambers (?) of the shrine (?) of Thoth?' Teta replied, 'No. I do not know their number, O king my lord, but I do know the place where they are to be found.' His Majesty asked, 'Where is that?' Teta replied, 'There is a box made of flint in a house called Sapti in Heliopolis.' The king asked, 'Who will bring me this box?' Teta replied, 'Behold, O king my lord, I shall not bring the box to thee.' His Majesty asked, 'Who then shall bring it to me?' Teta answered, 'The oldest of the three children of Rut-tetet shall bring it unto thee.' His Majesty said, 'It is my will that thou shalt tell me who this Rut-tetet is.' Teta answered, 'This Rut-tetet is the wife of a priest of Ra of Sakhabu, who is about to give birth to three children of Ra. He told her that these children should attain to the highest dignities in the whole country, and that the oldest of them should become high priest of Heliopolis.' On hearing these words the heart of the king became sad; and Teta said, 'Wherefore art thou so sad, O king my lord? Is it because of the three children? I say unto thee, Verily thy son, verily his son, verily one of them.' His Majesty asked, 'When will these three children be born?' Teta answered, 'Rut-tetet will give them birth on the fifteenth day of the first month of Pert.' The king then made a remark the exact meaning of which it is difficult to follow, but from one part of it it is clear that he expressed his determination to go and visit the temple of Ra of Sakhabu, which seems to have been situated on or near the great canal of the Letopolite nome. In reply Teta declared that he would take care that the water in the canal should be 4 cubits (about 6 feet) deep, i.e. that the water should be deep enough for the royal barge to sail on the canal without difficulty. The king then returned to his palace and gave orders that Teta should have lodgings given him in the house of Prince Herutataf, that he should live with him, and that he should be provided with one thousand bread-cakes, one hundred pots of beer, one ox, and one hundred bundles of vegetables. And all that the king commanded concerning Teta was done.

THE STORY OF TUT-TET-TET AND THE THREE SONS OF RA

When the day drew nigh in which the three sons were to be born, Ra, the Sun-god, ordered the four goddesses, Isis, Nephthys, Meskhenet, and Heqet, and the god Khnemu, to go and superintend the birth of the three children, so that when they grew up, and were exercising the functions of rule throughout all Egypt, they should build temples to them, and furnish the altars in them with offerings of meat and drink in abundance. Then the four goddesses changed themselves into the forms of dancing women, and went to the house wherein the lady Rut-tetet lay ill, and finding her husband, the priest of Ra, who was called Rauser, outside, they clashed their cymbals together, and rattled their sistra, and tried to make him merry. When Rauser objected to this and told them that his wife lay ill inside the house, they replied, 'Let us see her, for we know how to help her'; so he said to them and to Khnemu who was with them, 'Enter in,' and they did so, and they went to the room wherein Rut-tetet lay. Isis, Nephthys, and Heqet assisted in bringing the three boys into the world. Meskhenet prophesied for each of them sovereignty over the land, and Khnemu bestowed health upon their bodies. After the birth of the three boys, the four goddesses and Khnemu went outside the house, and told Rauser to rejoice because his wife Rut-tetet had given him three children. Rauser said, 'My Ladies, what can I do for you in return for this?' Having apparently nothing else to give them, he begged them to have barley brought from his granary, so that they might take it away as a gift to their own granaries; they agreed, and the god Khnemu brought the barley. So the goddesses set out to go to the place whence they had come.

When they had arrived there Isis said to her companions: 'How is it that we who went to Rut-tetet [by the command of Ra] have worked no wonder for the children which we could have announced to their father, who allowed us to depart [without begging a boon]?' So they made divine crowns such as belonged to the Lord (i.e. King), life, strength, health [be to him!], and they hid them in the barley. Then they sent rain and storm through the heavens, and they went back to the house of Rauser, apparently carrying the barley with them, and said to him, 'Let the barley abide in a sealed room until we dance our way back to the north.' So they put the barley in a sealed room. After Rut-tetet had kept herself secluded for fourteen days, she said to one of her handmaidens, 'Is the house all ready?' and the handmaiden told her that it was provided with everything except jars of barley drink, which had not been brought. Rut-tetet then asked why they had not been brought, and the handmaiden replied in words that seem to mean that there was no barley in the house except that which belonged to the dancing goddesses, and that that was in a chamber which had been sealed with their seal. Rut-tetet then told her to go and fetch some of the barley, for she was quite certain that when her husband Rauser returned he would make good what she took. Thereupon the handmaiden went to the chamber, and broke it open, and she heard in it loud cries and shouts, and the sounds of music and singing and dancing, and all the noises which men make in honour of the birth of a king, and she went back and told Rut-tetet what she had heard. Then Rut-tetet herself went through the room, and could not find the place where the noises came from, but when she laid her temple against a box, she perceived that the noises were inside it. She then took this box, which cannot have been of any great size, and put it in another box, which in turn she put in another box, which she sealed, and then wrapping this in a leather covering, she laid it in a chamber containing her jar of barley beer or barley wine, and sealed the door. When Rauser returned from the fields, Rut-tetet related to him everything that had happened, and his heart was exceedingly glad, and he and his wife sat down and enjoyed themselves.

A few days after these events Rut-tetet had a quarrel with her handmaiden, and she slapped her well. The handmaiden was very angry, and in the presence of the household she said words to this effect: Dost thou dare to treat me in this way? I who can destroy thee? She has given birth to three kings, and I will go and tell the Majesty of King Khufu of this fact. The handmaiden thought that, if Khufu knew of the views of Rauser and Rut-tetet about the future of their three sons, and the prophecies of the goddesses, he would kill the children and perhaps their parents also. With the object in her mind of telling the king the handmaiden went to her maternal uncle, whom she found weaving flax on the walk, and told him what had happened, and said she was going to tell the king about the three children. From her uncle she obtained neither support nor sympathy; on the contrary, gathering together several strands of flax into a thick rope he gave her a good beating with the same. A little later the handmaiden went to the river or canal to fetch some water, and whilst she was filling her pot a crocodile seized her and carried her away and, presumably, ate her. Then the uncle went to the house of Rut-tetet to tell her what had happened, and he found her sitting down, with her head bowed over her breast, and exceedingly sad and miserable. He asked her, saying, 'O Lady, wherefore art thou so sad?' And she told him that the cause of her sorrow was the handmaiden, who had been born in the house and had grown up in it, and who had just left it, threatening that she would go and tell the king about the birth of the three kings. The uncle of the handmaiden nodded his head in a consoling manner, and told Rut-tetet how she had come to him and informed him what she was going to do, and how he had given her a good beating with a rope of flax, and how she had gone to the river to fetch some water, and how a crocodile had carried her off.

There is reason to think that the three sons of Rut-tetet became the three kings of the Vth Dynasty who were known by the names of KhāfRa, MenkauRa, and Userkaf. The stories given above are valuable because they contain elements of history, for it is now well known that the immediate successors of the IVth Dynasty, of which Khufu, KhāfRa, and MenkauRa, the builders of the three great pyramids at Giza, were the most important kings, were kings who delighted to call themselves sons of Ra, and who spared no effort to make the form of worship of the Sun-god that was practised at Anu, or Heliopolis, universal in Egypt. It is probable that the three magicians, Ubaaner, Tchatchamānkh, and Teta were historical personages, whose abilities and skill in working magic appealed to the imagination of the Egyptians under all dynasties, and caused their names to be venerated to a remote posterity.

THE TRUE HISTORY OF SETNA

Edited by Lewis Spence

This story was discovered written on some papyrus belonging to the British Museum. An English translation was published in 1900 by Mr F. Ll. Griffith, and one in French by Sir G. Maspero in 1901. It is written on the back of some official documents in Greek and dates from the seventh year of the Emperor Claudian. The papyrus is much dilapidated and pasted end to end; it is incomplete, and the beginning of the history has disappeared. By the writing one would judge the copy to belong to the latter half of the second century of our era.

Once upon a time there was a king called Ousimares, and he had a son called Setna. This son was a scribe; he was clever with his hands, indeed in all things, and he excelled all men of the world learned in the arts or those among the renowned scribes of Egypt. It happened that the chiefs of certain foreign lands sent a message to Pharaoh challenging him to find one who would do such and such a thing under certain conditions. If this were done, then these chiefs would acknowledge the inferiority of their country to Egypt; but if, on the other hand, neither scribe nor wise man could accomplish it, then they would proclaim the inferiority of Egypt. Now Ousimares called his son Setna and repeated these words to him, and immediately Setna gave the answer to that which the chiefs had propounded, so that the latter were forced to carry out the conditions and admit the superiority of Egypt. And thus were they robbed of their triumph, so great was the wisdom of Setna, and none other ever dared to send such messages to Pharaoh.

Now Setna and his wife Mahîtouaskhît were greatly grieved, for they had no son. One day when he was troubled more than usual over this his wife went to the temple of Imhetep, and she prayed before him, saying, 'Turn thy face to me, O Imhetep, son of Ptah, thou who workest miracles, who art beneficent in all thy doings. It is thou who canst give a son to those who are sonless. Oh, hear my prayer, and grant that I shall bear a son!' And that night Mahîtouaskhît slept in the temple, and there she dreamed a dream wherein she was directed to prepare a magical remedy, and told that by this means her desire for a son should be fulfilled. On waking she did all according to her dream, and in time it was known that a child was to be born to her and Setna, who told it before Pharaoh with great joy, while to his wife, for her protection, he gave an amulet and put spells about her.

And one night Setna dreamed, and a voice said to him, 'Mahîtouaskhît, thy wife, will bring forth a son, and through him many wonders shall be accomplished in the land of Egypt. And the name of thy son shall be Se-Osiris.' When Setna awoke and remembered these words he rejoiced and was glad in heart.

In due time a son was born, and according to the dream he was called Se-Osiris. And the child developed rapidly beyond all other children, and Setna loved him so greatly that scarce an hour passed without his seeing him. In time he was put to school, but soon showed that he knew more than the tutor could teach him. He began to read the magical papyri with the priestly scribes in the 'Double House of Life' of the temple of Ptah, and all those about him were lost in astonishment. Then was Setna so pleased that he led his son before Pharaoh to the festival that all the magicians of the king might strive against him and have to acknowledge their defeat.

And one day, when Setna, together with the boy Se-Osiris, was preparing for the festival, loud voices of lamentation rose upon the air, and Setna, looking forth from the terrace of his apartments, saw the body of a rich man being carried to the mountains for burial with great honour and loud wailing. Again he looked forth, and this time he saw the body of a peasant borne along wrapped in a mat of straw and without a soul to mourn him. And seeing this Setna exclaimed, 'By the life of Osiris, god of Amenti, may it be that I come into Amenti as this rich man comes, honoured and lamented, and not as the peasant, alone and already forgotten!' Upon hearing this Se-Osiris said, 'Nay, my father, rather may the fate of the poor man be thine, and not that of the rich one!' Setna was astonished and hurt at this and cried, 'Are they the words of a son who loves his father?' Se-Osiris answered him: 'My father, I will show to thee each in his place, the peasant unwept and the rich man so lamented.'

Then Setna demanded of him how he could accomplish this. The child Se-Osiris began to recite words from the magical books, words of power. Next he took his father by the hand and led him to an unknown place in the mountains of Memphis. Here there were seven great halls filled with people of all conditions. They traversed three of these without hindrance. Upon entering the fourth Setna saw a mass of men who rushed hither and thither, writhing as creatures attacked them from behind; others, famished, were springing and jumping in their efforts to reach the food suspended above them, whilst some, again, dug holes at their feet to prevent them attaining their object. In the fifth hall were venerable shades who had each found their proper and fitting place, but those who were accused of crimes lingered kneeling at the door, which pivoted upon the eye of a man who ceaselessly prayed and groaned. In the sixth hall were the gods of Amenti, who sat in council, each in his place, whilst the keepers of the portals called out the causes. In the seventh hall was seated the great god Osiris on a golden throne, crowned with the plumed diadem. On his left was Anubis, and on his right the god Thoth. In the midst were the scales wherein were weighed the faults and virtues of the souls of the dead, while Thoth wrote down the judgment that Anubis pronounced. Then those whose faults outweighed their virtues were delivered to Amait, the attendant of the Lord of Amenti; their souls and bodies were destroyed for ever. But those whose virtues were greater than their failings took their place among the gods and shades, and there their souls found a heaven. Those, again, whose merits and faults were equal were put amongst the servitors of Sekerosiris.

Then Setna saw near the place of Osiris one of exalted rank and robed in the finest linen. And while Setna was marvelling at all he had seen in the land of Amenti, Se-Osiris, his little son, said unto him, 'My father Setna, seest thou that great personage in fine robes and near to Osiris? That peasant whom thou didst see carried out of Memphis without a soul to accompany him, and his body wrapped in a mat, dost thou remember, my father? Well, that peasant is the one beside Osiris! When he had come to Amenti and they weighed his faults and virtues, lo! his virtues outweighed all. And by the judgment of the gods all the honours that had been the share of the rich man were given to the peasant, and by the law of Osiris he takes his place midst the honoured and exalted. But the rich man, when he had come to Hades and his merits were weighed, lo! his faults weighed heavier, and he is that man you have seen upon whose eye pivots the door of the fifth hall, the man who cries and prays aloud with great agony. By the life of Osiris, god of Amenti, if upon earth I said to thee, "Rather may the fate of the peasant be thine than that of the rich man," it was because I knew their fates, my father.'

And Setna answered and said, 'My son Se-Osiris, numberless marvels have I seen in Amenti; but tell me the meaning of those people we saw rushing before creatures who devoured them, and the others ever trying to reach the food beyond their reach.'

Se-Osiris answered him:

'In truth, my father, they are under the curse of the gods; they are those who upon earth wasted their substance, and the creatures who devour them without ceasing are the women with whom they squandered both life and substance, and now they have naught, though they should work day and night. And so it is with all: as they have been on earth, so it is with them in Amenti, according to their good and bad deeds. That is the immutable law of the gods, the law that knows no change and under which all men must come when they enter Hades.'

Then Setna and his son returned hand in hand from the mountains of Memphis. A fear was upon Setna because of Se-Osiris, who answered not, and then he pronounced words that exorcize the ghosts of the dead. Always afterward he remembered all he had seen and marvelled thereat, but spoke of it to no man. And when Se-Osiris was twelve years of age there was no scribe or magician in Memphis who was his equal in the reading of the magical books.

After this it happened one day that the Pharaoh Ousimares was seated in the Hall of Audience with the princes, the military chiefs, and the nobles of Egypt, each according to his rank, gathered about him. One said unto Pharaoh, 'Here is a rascally Ethiopian who would fain have speech with you and who carries a sealed letter.' And Pharaoh commanded that the man be brought before him. And when he was come he made obeisance and said, 'Here is a sealed letter which I bear, and I would fain know if amongst your wise men there are any who can read its contents without breaking the seals. If, O king, you have not such a one among your scribes and magicians, I shall take back to my country, the land of the Negro, the story of Egypt's failure and inferiority.' Upon hearing these words all were amazed, and those about the king exclaimed loudly, while Pharaoh bade some bring to him his son Setna. When he had come, instantly obeying the royal command and bowing low before him, Pharaoh said, 'My son Setna, hast thou heard the words of this insolent Ethiopian?' and then he repeated the challenge. Then was Setna astonished, but he answered immediately, 'Great Lord, who can read a letter without its being opened and spread before him? But if you will give me ten days, I will think upon it and do what I can to avoid the report of Egypt's failure being carried to the Negroes, eaters of gum.' And Pharaoh said, 'Those days are granted, my son.' Then were rooms appointed for the Ethiopian, and Pharaoh rose from his palace sad at heart and went fasting to his couch.

And Setna, pondering and much disturbed, threw himself upon his couch, but knew no rest. His wife Mahîtouaskhît came to him and would fain have shared his trouble, but he said that it was not for a woman to share or one that she might help him in. Later, his son Se-Osiris came and begged to know what so sorely troubled his father, and again Setna refused to speak, saying that it was not for a child. But the boy persisted, and at last Setna told him of the challenge of the Ethiopian. The moment he had finished Se-Osiris laughed, and his father asked the reason of his mirth.

'My father,' he answered, 'I laugh to see you there, so troubled in heart because of such a small affair. I will read that letter of the Ethiopian, read it all without breaking the seals.'

Hearing this, Setna rose instantly.

'But what proof can you give me of the truth of what you say, my son?'

Se-Osiris answered, 'My father, go thou to the lower floor of this house and take what books you please from their place. As you do so I shall read that which you have taken from its place while I stand before you.'

And it happened as Se-Osiris had said. Each book that his father lifted the boy read without its being opened. Upon this Setna lost no time in acquainting Pharaoh with all that Se-Osiris had done, and so lightened was the heart of the king that he made a feast in honour of Setna and his young son.

After this Pharaoh sent for the Ethiopian. And when he entered the Hall of Audience he was placed in the midst of all, and the young Se-Osiris took up his place beside him. But first the boy put a curse upon the man and his gods if he should dare to say falsely that what he read was not true. And seeing the boy, the Ethiopian prostrated himself before him in fear. Then Se-Osiris began to read the letter with its seals still unbroken, and all heard his voice. And the words were:

'It happened during the reign of the Pharaoh Manakhphrê-Siamon, who was a beneficent ruler and in whose time the land overflowed with all good things, who endowed the temples richly, that when the King of Nubia was taking his rest in the pleasure-kiosk of Amen he overheard the voices of three Ethiopians who were talking behind the house. One of them was speaking in a high voice, saying, among other things, that if the god Amen would preserve him from the enmity of the King of Egypt he could put a spell on the people of that country so that a great darkness should reign and they should not see the moon for three days and three nights. Then the second man said that if Amen would guard him he would cause the Pharaoh to be transported to the land of the Negroes, and there, before the king of that country and in public, he should suffer five hundred blows, and afterward he should be taken back to his country in not more than six hours. After this the third man spoke, saying that if Amen would preserve him he would then send a blight upon the land of Egypt, a blight for the space of three years. When the king heard this he ordered that these three men be brought before him.

'He said unto them, "Which of you said that he would cause that the people of Egypt should not see the moon for three days and three nights?" And they answered that it was Horus, the son of Tririt (the sow).

'Again the king said, "Which of you said that he had power to cause the King of Egypt to be brought hither?" And they answered that it was Horus, the son of Tnahsit.

'Again the king said, "Which of you said that he would cause a blight to fall upon Egypt?" And they answered that it was Horus, the son of Triphît (the princess).

'Then the king bade Horus, the son of Tnahsit, come near, and he said to him, "By Amen, the Bull of Meroe, if thou canst accomplish what thou hast said, then rich rewards shall be thine."

'And Horus, the son of Tnahsit, fashioned a litter and four bearers of wax. Over them he chanted magical words, he breathed upon them and gave them life, and finally he bade them wend their way to Egypt and bring back the king of that land in order that he might suffer five hundred blows from the kourbash before the King of the Negroes.'

Here Se-Osiris paused and, turning to the Ethiopian, said, 'The curse of Amen fall upon thee! These words that I have said, are they not written in the letter thou holdest in thine hand?' And the rascally Ethiopian bowed low before him, saying, 'They are written there, my lord!'

Then Se-Osiris resumed his magical reading:

'And all happened as Horus, the son of Tnahsit, had devised. By the power of sorcery was Pharaoh taken to the land of the Negroes, and there suffered five hundred blows of the kourbash. After that he was carried back to Egypt, as had been said, and, wakening the next morning in the temple of the god Horus, he lay in great pain, his body sorely bruised. Bewildered, he asked his courtiers how such could have happened in Egypt. They, thinking some madness had fallen upon their king, and yet ashamed of their thoughts, spoke soothingly to him, and said that the great gods would heal his afflictions. But still they asked him the meaning of his strange words, and suddenly he remembered all that had happened to him and recounted it to his courtiers.'

'When they saw his bruised body they made a great clamour. And then Pharaoh sent for his chief magician, and he at once cried out that the evil and affliction of the king were due to the sorceries of the Ethiopians.

'"By the life of Ptah," he continued, "I shall bring them to torture and execution."

'And Pharaoh bade him make all speed lest he should be carried away the next night. And the chief magician carried his secret books and amulets to the place where Pharaoh lay, and chanted above him magical words and incantations. Then, with many gifts, he embarked in a boat and made haste to reach the temple of Khmounon, and there he prayed to the god Thoth that all evil should be averted from Pharaoh and the land of Egypt. And that night he slept in the temple, and he dreamed a dream in which the god Thoth appeared to him and instructed him in divine magic that would preserve the king from the wiles of the Ethiopians.

'On waking the magician remembered all, and without losing a moment fulfilled all that he had been told in his dream. And then he wrote the charm to preserve Pharaoh from all sorcery. On the second day the Ethiopians endeavoured to renew their enchantments, but all was now unavailing against the person of Pharaoh. The third morning Pharaoh recounted to his chief musicians all that had happened during the night, and how the Ethiopians had failed in their attempts.

'Then the magician fashioned a litter and four bearers of wax. He put a spell upon them and breathed life into them, bidding them go and bring before Pharaoh the King of the Negroes, that he might suffer five hundred blows upon his body and then be carried back to his own land again. And the waxen figures promised to do all as the magician had commanded.'

Again Se-Osiris paused, and again he demanded of the Ethiopian if his words were not the words of the sealed letter. And the Ethiopian bowed low to the ground, saying they were the words in very truth.

Se-Osiris began again to read the hidden words:

'And as it happened to Pharaoh, so was the fate of the King of the Negroes, who awoke sorely bruised in the morning following. He called loudly for his, and when they saw the state of their king they made a great clamour. Again he called and commanded that Horus, the son of Tnahsit, be brought before him. When he had come the king threatened him, and commanded him to go to Egypt and there learn how to save him from the sorceries of Pharaoh's chief magician.

'But no spell devised by the Ethiopian could preserve the king from the magic of the Egyptians, and three times was he carried to that country and humiliated, whilst his body was in great pain, so sorely bruised was it. Then he cursed Horus, the son of Tnahsit, and threatened him with a slow and dreadful death unless he could preserve him from Pharaoh's vengeance.

'Then in fear and trouble Horus went to his mother Tnahsit and told her all, and that he must go to Egypt to see the one who had worked these powerful sorceries and endeavour to inflict upon him a fitting punishment. And his mother, Tnahsit, on hearing this, warned him against coming into the presence of Pharaoh's chief magician, for against him he would never prevail, but know defeat. But he answered that he must go. Then she arranged with him that by signs and signals between them he should let her know how he fared, and if he were in danger, then she should try to save him. And he promised, saying that if he were vanquished, then that which she ate, that which she drank, and the sky above should turn to the colour of blood.

'And after this he journeyed to Egypt, tracking the one whose sorceries had prevailed against his own. He penetrated to the Royal Hall of Audience and came before Pharaoh, crying in a high voice, "Who is it among you who is putting spells upon me?"

'And Pharaoh's chief magician called out in answer, saying, "Ha! Ethiopian, is it thou who workedst evil against Pharaoh?" and Horus, the son of Tnahsit, cried out in great anger and by a spell he caused a great flame to rise from the midst of the hall, at which Pharaoh and the Egyptians cried out to the chief of the magicians to succour them. Then by his power he caused a shower of rain to fall so that the flame was extinguished.

'Again the Ethiopian wrought his magic and thereby caused a great darkness to fall upon them all so that the people could not see each other, but this also was dispersed by the magician of the Egyptians. Then followed more machinations by Horus, the son of Tnahsit, but each time was he vanquished. At last he asked for mercy and vowed before the gods that never again would he trouble Egypt or Pharaoh. They gave him a boat and sent him back to his own land. So were the sorceries of the Ethiopians rendered as naught.'

With this Se-Osiris finished the reading of the sealed letter. And then he began to reveal to all there, Pharaoh, the princes, and the nobles, that the Ethiopian now before them was none other than that Horus, son of Tnahsit, returned after five hundred years to trouble Egypt and its king again. But against this day he himself, Se-Osiris, had been born again, for he was that former chief magician of the Pharaoh Manakhphrê come back once more to protect Egypt and Pharaoh from the wiles of the Ethiopians.

And with these words he caused a great flame to consume the Ethiopian, there in the midst of the Hall of Audience, so that not a vestige of the creature remained. But afterward when they looked for Se-Osiris he had disappeared as a shadow from before Pharaoh and his father Setna, and never again was he seen of them.

At these happenings everyone marvelled, and Pharaoh said that Se-Osiris was the wisest and most wonderful of all magicians, and that never again would the world see his like.

But the hearts of Setna and his wife were troubled, and they grieved sorely for their son Se-Osiris. Then comfort came to them, and again the wife of Setna bore a son, and they called him Ousimanthor. And so the heart of Setna was glad and he made offerings in the name of Se-Osiris in remembrance.

SETNA AND THE MAGIC BOOK

Translated by W. M. Flinders Petrie

This tale of Setna only exists in one copy, a demotic papyrus in the Giza Museum. Unhappily the opening of this tale is lost, and I have therefore restored it by a recital of the circumstances which are referred to in what remains. We must remember that it was written in the Ptolemaic period concerning an age long past. Five different acts, as we may call them, succeed one another. In the first act – which is entirely lost, and here only outlined – the circumstances which led Setna of the XIXth Dynasty to search for the magic book must have been related. In the second act Ahura recites the long history of herself and family, to deter Setna from his purpose. This act is a complete tale by itself, and belongs to a time some generations before Setna; it is here supposed to belong to the time of Amenhotep III, in the details of costume adopted for illustration. The third act is Setna's struggle as a rival magician to Na-nefer-ka-ptah, from which he finally comes off victorious by his brother's use of a talisman, and so secures possession of the coveted magic book. The fourth act – which I have here only summarised – shows how Na-nefer-ka-ptah resorts to a bewitchment of Setna by a sprite, by subjection to whom he loses his magic power. The fifth act shows Setna as subjected to Na-nefer-ka-ptah, and ordered by him to bring the bodies of his wife and child to Memphis into his tomb. While, therefore, the sentimental climax of the tale – the restoration of the unity of the family in one tomb – belongs to persons of the XVIIIth Dynasty, the action of the tale is entirely of the XIXth Dynasty, for what happened in the XVIIIth Dynasty (second act) is all related in the XIXth.

The mighty King User-maat-ra (Rameses the Great) had a son named Setna Kha-em-uast who was a great scribe, and very learned in all the ancient writings. And he heard that the magic book of Thoth, by which a man may enchant heaven and earth, and know the language of all birds and beasts, was buried in the cemetery of Memphis. And he went to search for it with his brother An-he-hor-eru; and when they found the tomb of the king's son, Na-nefer-ka-ptah, son of the king of Upper and Lower Egypt, Mer-neb-ptah, Setna opened it and went in.

Now in the tomb was Na-nefer-ka-ptah, and with him was the ka of his wife Ahura; for though she was buried at Koptos, her ka dwelt at Memphis with her husband, whom she loved. And Setna saw them seated before their offerings, and the book lay between them. And Na-nefer-ka-ptah said to Setna, 'Who are you that break into my tomb in this way?' He said, 'I am Setna, son of the great King User-maat-ra, living for ever, and I come for that book which I see between you.' And Na-nefer-ka-ptah said, 'It cannot be given to you.' Then said Setna, 'But I will carry it away by force.'

Then Ahura said to Setna, 'Do not take this book; for it will bring trouble on you, as it has upon us. Listen to what we have suffered for it.'

AHURA'S TALE

'We were the two children of the King Mer-neb-ptah, and he loved us very much, for he had no others; and Na-nefer-ka-ptah was in his palace as heir over all the land. And when we were grown, the king said to the queen, "I will marry Na-nefer-ka-ptah to the daughter of a general, and Ahura to the son of another general." And the queen said, "No, he is the heir, let him marry his sister, like the heir of a king, none other is fit for him." And the king said, "That is not fair; they had better be married to the children of the general."

'And the queen said, "It is you who are not dealing rightly with me." And the king answered, "If I have no more than these two children, is it right that they should marry one another? I will marry Na-nefer-ka-ptah to the daughter of an officer, and Ahura to the son of another officer. It has often been done so in our family."

'And at a time when there was a great feast before the king, they came to fetch me to the feast. And I was very troubled, and did not behave as I used to do. And the king said to me, "Ahura, have you sent some one to me about this sorry matter, saying, 'Let me be married to my elder brother'?" I said to him, "Well, let me marry the son of an officer, and he marry the daughter of another officer, as it often happens so in our family." I laughed, and the king laughed. And the king told the steward of the palace, "Let them take Ahura to the house of Na-nefer-ka-ptah to-night, and all kinds of good things with her." So they brought me as a wife to the house of Na-nefer-ka-ptah; and the king ordered them to give me presents of silver and gold, and things from the palace.

'And Na-nefer-ka-ptah passed a happy time with me, and received all the presents from the palace; and we loved one another. And when I expected a child, they told the king, and he was most heartily glad; and he sent me many things, and a present of the best silver and gold and linen. And when the time came, I bore this little child that is before you. And they gave him the name of Mer-ab, and registered him in the book of the 'House of life.'

'And when my brother Na-nefer-ka-ptah went to the cemetery of Memphis, he did nothing on earth but read the writings that are in the catacombs of the kings, and the tablets of the 'House of life,' and the inscriptions that are seen on the monuments, and he worked hard on the writings. And there was a priest there called Nesi-ptah; and as Na-nefer-ka-ptah went into a temple to pray, it happened that he went behind this priest, and was reading the inscriptions that were on the chapels of the gods. And the priest mocked him and laughed. So Na-nefer-ka-ptah said to him, "Why are you laughing at me?" And he replied, "I was not laughing at you, or if I happened to do so, it was at your reading writings that are worthless. If you wish so much to read writings, come to me, and I will bring you to the place where the book is which Thoth himself wrote with his own hand, and which will bring you to the gods. When you read but two pages in this you will enchant the heaven, the earth, the abyss, the mountains, and the sea; you shall know what the birds of the sky and the crawling things are saying; you shall see the fishes of the deep, for a divine power is there to bring them up out of the depth. And when you read the second page, if you are in the world of ghosts, you will become again in the shape you were in on earth. You will see the sun shining in the sky, with all the gods, and the full moon."

'And Na-nefer-ka-ptah said, "By the life of the king! Tell me of anything you want done and I'll do it for you, if you will only send me where this book is." And the priest answered Na-nefer-ka-ptah, "If you want to go to the place where the book is, you must give me a hundred pieces of silver for my funeral, and provide that they shall bury me as a rich priest." So Na-nefer-ka-ptah called his lad and told him to give the priest a hundred pieces of silver; and he made them do as he wished, even everything that he asked for. Then the priest said to Na-nefer-ka-ptah, "This book is in the middle of the river at Koptos, in an iron box; in the iron box is a bronze box; in the bronze box is a sycamore box; in the sycamore box is an ivory and ebony box; in the ivory and ebony box is a silver box; in the silver box is a golden box, and in that is the book.

It is twisted all round with snakes and scorpions and all the other crawling things around the box in which the book is; and there is a deathless snake by the box." And when the priest told Na-nefer-ka-ptah, he did not know where on earth he was, he was so much delighted.

'And when he came from the temple he told me all that had happened to him. And he said, "I shall go to Koptos, for I must fetch this book; I will not stay any longer in the north." And I said, "Let me dissuade you, for you prepare sorrow and you will bring me into trouble in the Thebaid." And I laid my hand on Na-nefer-ka-ptah, to keep him from going to Koptos, but he would not listen to me; and he went to the king, and told the king all that the priest had said. The king asked him, "What is it that you want?" and he replied, "Let them give me the royal boat with its belongings, for I will go to the south with Ahura and her little boy Mer-ab, and fetch this book without delay." So they gave him the royal boat with its belongings, and we went with him to the haven, and sailed from there up to Koptos.

'Then the priests of Isis of Koptos, and the high priest of Isis, came down to us without waiting, to meet Na-nefer-ka-ptah, and their wives also came to me. We went into the temple of Isis and Harpokrates; and Na-nefer-ka-ptah brought an ox, a goose, and some wine, and made a burnt-offering and a drink-offering before Isis of Koptos and Harpokrates. They brought us to a very fine house, with all good things; and Na-nefer-ka-ptah spent four days there and feasted with the priests of Isis of Koptos, and the wives of the priests of Isis also made holiday with me.

'And the morning of the fifth day came; and Na-nefer-ka-ptah called a priest to him, and made a magic cabin that was full of men and tackle. He put the spell upon it, and put life in it, and gave them breath, and sank it in the water. He filled the royal boat with sand, and took leave of me, and sailed from the haven: and I sat by the river at Koptos that I might see what would become of him. And he said, "Workmen, work for me, even at the place where the book is." And they toiled by night and by day; and when they had reached it in three days, he threw the sand out, and made a shoal in the river. And then he found on it entwined serpents and scorpions and all kinds of crawling things around the box in which the book was; and by it he found a deathless snake around the box. And he laid the spell upon the entwined serpents and scorpions and all kinds of crawling things which were around the box, that they should not come out. And he went to the deathless snake, and fought with him, and killed him; but he came to life again, and took a new form. He then fought again with him a second time; but he came to life again, and took a third form. He then cut him in two parts, and put sand between the parts, that he should not appear again.

'Na-nefer-ka-ptah then went to the place where he found the box. He uncovered a box of iron, and opened it; he found then a box of bronze, and opened that; then he found a box of sycamore wood, and opened that; again, he found a box of ivory and ebony, and opened that; yet, he found a box of silver, and opened that; and then he found a box of gold; he opened that, and found the book in it. He took the book from the golden box, and read a page of spells from it. He enchanted the heaven and the earth, the abyss, the mountains, and the sea; he knew what the birds of the sky, the fish of the deep, and the beasts of the hills all said. He read another page of the spells, and saw the sun shining in the sky, with all the gods, the full moon, and the stars in their shapes; he saw the fishes of the deep, for a divine power was present that brought them up from the water. He then read the spell upon the workmen that he had made, and taken from the haven, and said to them, "Work for me, back to the place from which I came." And they toiled night and day, and so he came back to the place where I sat by the river of Koptos; I had not drunk nor eaten anything, and had done nothing on earth, but sat like one who is gone to the grave.

'I then told Na-nefer-ka-ptah that I wished to see this book, for which we had taken so much trouble. He gave the book into my hands; and when I read a page of the spells in it I also enchanted heaven and earth, the abyss, the mountains, and the sea; I also knew what the birds of the sky, the fishes of the deep, and the beasts of the hills all said. I read another page of the spells, and I saw the sun shining in the sky with all the gods, the full moon, and the stars in their shapes; I saw the fishes of the deep, for a divine power was present that brought them up from the water. As I could not write, I asked Na-nefer-ka-ptah, who was a good writer, and a very learned one; he called for a new piece of papyrus, and wrote on it all that was in the book before him. He dipped it in beer, and washed it off in the liquid; for he knew that if it were washed off, and he drank it, he would know all that there was in the writing.

'We returned back to Koptos the same day, and made a feast before Isis of Koptos and Harpokrates. We then went to the haven and sailed, and went northward of Koptos. And as we went on Thoth discovered all that Na-nefer-ka-ptah had done with the book; and Thoth hastened to tell Ra, and said, "Now know that my book and my revelation are with Na-nefer-ka-ptah, son of the King Mer-neb-ptah. He has forced himself into my place, and robbed it, and seized my box with the writings, and killed my guards who protected it." And Ra replied to him, "He is before you, take him and all his kin." He sent a power from heaven with the command, "Do not let Na-nefer-ka-ptah return safe to Memphis with all his kin." And after this hour, the little boy Mer-ab, going out from the awning of the royal boat, fell into the river: he called on Ra, and everybody who was on the bank raised a cry. Na-nefer-ka-ptah went out of the cabin, and read the spell over him; he brought his body up because a divine power brought him to the surface. He read another spell over him, and made him tell of all what happened to him, and of what Thoth had said before Ra.

'We turned back with him to Koptos. We brought him to the Good House, we fetched the people to him, and made one embalm him; and we buried him in his coffin in the cemetery of Koptos like a great and noble person.

'And Na-nefer-ka-ptah, my brother, said, "Let us go down, let us not delay, for the king has not yet heard of what has happened to him, and his heart will be sad about it." So we went to the haven, we sailed, and did not stay to the north of Koptos. When we were come to the place where the little boy Mer-ab had fallen in the water, I went out from the awning of the royal boat, and I fell into the river. They called Na-nefer-ka-ptah, and he came out from the cabin of the royal boat; he read a spell over me, and brought my body up, because a divine power brought me to the surface. He drew me out, and read the spell over me, and made me tell him of all that had happened to me, and of what Thoth had said before Ra. Then he turned back with me to Koptos, he brought me to the Good House, he fetched the people to me, and made one embalm me, as great and noble people are buried, and laid me in the tomb where Mer-ab my young child was.

'He turned to the haven, and sailed down, and delayed not in the north of Koptos. When he was come to the place where we fell into the river, he said to his heart, "Shall I not better turn back again to Koptos, that I may lie by them? For, if not, when I go down to Memphis, and the king asks after his children, what shall I say to him? Can I tell him, 'I have taken your children to the Thebaid, and killed them, while I remained alive, and I have come to Memphis still alive'?" Then he made them bring him a linen cloth of striped byssus; he made a band, and bound the book firmly, and tied it upon him. Na-nefer-ka-ptah then went out of the awning of the royal boat and fell into the river. He cried on Ra; and all those who were on the bank made an outcry, saying, "Great woe! Sad woe! Is he lost, that good scribe and able man that has no equal?"

'The royal boat went on, without any one on earth knowing where Na-nefer-ka-ptah was. It went on to Memphis, and they told all this to the king. Then the king went down to the royal boat in mourning, and all the soldiers and high priests and priests of Ptah were in mourning, and all the officials and courtiers. And when he saw Na-nefer-ka-ptah, who was in the inner cabin of the royal boat – from his rank of high scribe – he lifted him up. And they saw the book by him; and the king said, "Let one hide this book that is with him." And the officers of the king, the priests of Ptah, and the high priest of Ptah, said to the king, "Our Lord, may the king live as long as the sun! Na-nefer-ka-ptah was a good scribe, and a very skilful man." And the king had him laid in his Good House to the sixteenth day, and then had him wrapped to the thirty-fifth day, and laid him out to the seventieth day, and then had him put in his grave in his resting-place.

'I have now told you the sorrow which has come upon us because of this book for which you ask, saying, "Let it be given to me." You have no claim to it; and, indeed, for the sake of it, we have given up our life on earth.'

***

And Setna said to Ahura, 'Give me the book which I see between you and Na-nefer-ka-ptah; for if you do not I will take it by force.' Then Na-nefer-ka-ptah rose from his seat and said, 'Are you Setna, to whom my wife has told of all these blows of fate, which you have not suffered? Can you take this book by your skill as a good scribe? If, indeed, you can play games with me, let us play a game, then, of 52 points.' And Setna said, 'I am ready,' and the board and its pieces were put before him. And Na-nefer-ka-ptah won a game from Setna; and he put the spell upon him, and defended himself with the game board that was before him, and sunk him into the ground above his feet. He did the same at the second game, and won it from Setna, and sunk him into the ground to his waist.

He did the same at the third game, and made him sink into the ground up to his ears. Then Setna struck Na-nefer-ka-ptah a great blow with his hand. And Setna called his brother An-he-hor-eru and said to him, 'Make haste and go up upon earth, and tell the king all that has happened to me, and bring me the talisman of my father Ptah, and my magic books.'

And he hurried up upon earth, and told the king all that had happened to Setna. The king said, 'Bring him the talisman of his father Ptah, and his magic books.' And An-he-hor-eru hurried down into the tomb; he laid the talisman on Setna, and he sprang up again immediately. And then Setna reached out his hand for the book, and took it. Then – as Setna went out from the tomb – there went a Light before him, and Darkness behind him. And Ahura wept at him, and she said, 'Glory to the King of Darkness! Hail to the King of Light! all power is gone from the tomb.' But Na-nefer-ka-ptah said to Ahura, 'Do not let your heart be sad; I will make him bring back this book, with a forked stick in his hand, and a fire-pan on his head.' And Setna went out from the tomb, and it closed behind him as it was before.

Then Setna went to the king, and told him everything that had happened to him with the book. And the king said to Setna, 'Take back the book to the grave of Na-nefer-ka-ptah, like a prudent man, or else he will make you bring it with a forked stick in your hand, and a fire-pan on your head.' But Setna would not listen to him; and when Setna had unrolled the book he did nothing on earth but read it to everybody.

[Here follows a story of how Setna, walking in the court of the temple of Ptah, met Tabubua, a fascinating girl, daughter of a priest of Bast, of Ankhtaui; how she repelled his advances, until she had beguiled him into giving up all his possessions, and slaying his children. At the last she gives a fearful cry and vanishes, leaving Setna bereft of even his clothes. This would seem to be merely a dream, by the disappearance of Tabubua, and by Setna finding his children alive after it all; but on the other hand he comes to his senses in an unknown place, and is so terrified as to be quite ready to make restitution to Na-nefer-ka-ptah. The episode, which is not creditable to Egyptian society, seems to be intended for one of the vivid dreams which the credulous readily accept as half realities.]

So Setna went to Memphis, and embraced his children for that they were alive. And the king said to him, 'Were you not drunk to do so?' Then Setna told all things that had happened with Tabubua and Na-nefer-ka-ptah. And the king said, 'Setna, I have already lifted up my hand against you before, and said, "He will kill you if you do not take back the book to the place you took it from." But you have never listened to me till this hour. Now, then, take the book to Na-nefer-ka-ptah, with a forked stick in your hand, and a fire-pan on your head.'

So Setna went out from before the king, with a forked stick in his hand, and a firepan on his head. He went down to the tomb in which was Na-nefer-ka-ptah. And Ahura said to him, 'It is Ptah, the great god, that has brought you back safe.' Na-nefer-ka-ptah laughed, and he said, 'This is the business that I told you before.' And when Setna had praised Na-nefer-ka-ptah, he found it as the proverb says, 'The sun was in the whole tomb.' And Ahura and Na-nefer-ka-ptah besought Setna greatly. And Setna said, 'Na-nefer-ka-ptah, is it aught disgraceful (that you lay on me to do)?' And Na-nefer-ka-ptah said, 'Setna, you know this, that Ahura and Mer-ab, her child, behold! they are in Koptos; bring them here into this tomb, by the skill of a good scribe. Let it be impressed upon you to take pains, and to go to Koptos to bring them here.' Setna then went out from the tomb to the king, and told the king all that Na-nefer-ka-ptah had told him.

The king said, 'Setna, go to Koptos and bring back Ahura and Mer-ab.' He answered the king, 'Let one give me the royal boat and its belongings.' And they gave him the royal boat and its belongings, and he left the haven, and sailed without stopping till he came to Koptos.

And they made this known to the priests of Isis at Koptos and to the high priest of Isis; and behold they came down to him, and gave him their hand to the shore. He went up with them and entered into the temple of Isis of Koptos and of Harpokrates. He ordered one to offer for him an ox, a goose, and some wine, and he made a burnt-offering and a drink-offering before Isis of Koptos and Harpokrates. He went to the cemetery of Koptos with the priests of Isis and the high priest of Isis. They dug about for three days and three nights, for they searched even in all the catacombs which were in the cemetery of Koptos; they turned over the steles of the scribes of the 'double house of life', and read the inscriptions that they found on them. But they could not find the resting-place of Ahura and Mer-ab.

Now Na-nefer-ka-ptah perceived that they could not find the resting-place of Ahura and her child Mer-ab. So he raised himself up as a venerable, very old, ancient, and came before Setna. And Setna saw him, and Setna said to the ancient, 'You look like a very old man, do you know where is the resting-place of Ahura and her child Mer-ab?' The ancient said to Setna, 'It was told by the father of the father of my father to the father of my father, and the father of my father has told it to my father; the resting-place of Ahura and of her child Mer-ab is in a mound south of the town of Pehemato (?).' And Setna said to the ancient, 'Perhaps we may do damage to Pehemato, and you are ready to lead one to the town for the sake of that.' The ancient replied to Setna, 'If one listens to me, shall he therefore destroy the town of Pehemato! If they do not find Ahura and her child Mer-ab under the south corner of their town may I be disgraced.' They attended to the ancient, and found the resting-place of Ahura and her child Mer-ab under the south corner of the town of Pehemato. Setna laid them in the royal boat to bring them as honoured persons, and restored the town of Pehemato as it originally was. And Na-nefer-ka-ptah made Setna to know that it was he who had come to Koptos, to enable them to find out where the resting-place was of Ahura and her child Mer-ab.

So Setna left the haven in the royal boat, and sailed without stopping, and reached Memphis with all the soldiers who were with him. And when they told the king he came down to the royal boat. He took them as honoured persons escorted to the catacombs, in which Na-nefer-ka-ptah was, and smoothed down the ground over them.

This is the completed writing of the tale of Setna Kha-em-uast, and Na-nefer-ka-ptah, and his wife Ahura, and their Mid Mer-ab. It was written in the 35th year, the month Tybi.

ANPU AND BATA

Edited by W. M. Flinders Petrie

This tale, which is perhaps, of all this series, the best known in modern times, has often been published. It exists only in one papyrus. The papyrus had belonged to Sety II when crown prince, and hence is of the XIXth Dynasty. The present translation is, however, a fresh one made by Mr Griffith word for word, and shaped as little as possible by myself in editing it. The author of Anpu and Bata ends with a curse: 'Written by the scribe Anena, the owner of this roll. He who speaks against this roll, may Tahuti smite him.'

Once there were two brethren, of one mother and one father; Anpu was the name of the elder, and Bata was the name of the younger. Now, as for Anpu he had a house, and he had a wife. But his little brother was to him as it were a son; he it was who made for him his clothes; he it was who followed behind his oxen to the fields; he it was who did the ploughing; he it was who harvested the corn; he it was who did for him all the matters that were in the field. Behold, his younger brother grew to be an excellent worker, there was not his equal in the whole land; behold, the spirit of a god was in him.

Now after this the younger brother followed his oxen in his daily manner; and every evening he turned again to the house, laden with all the herbs of the field, with milk and with wood, and with all things of the field. And he put them down before his elder brother, who was sitting with his wife; and he drank and ate, and he lay down in his stable with the cattle. And at the dawn of day he took bread which he had baked, and laid it before his elder brother; and he took with him his bread to the field, and he drove his cattle to pasture in the fields. And as he walked behind his cattle, they said to him, 'Good is the herbage which is in that place;' and he listened to all that they said, and he took them to the good place which they desired. And the cattle which were before him became exceeding excellent, and they multiplied greatly.

Now at the time of ploughing his elder brother said unto him, 'Let us make ready for ourselves a goodly yoke of oxen for ploughing, for the land has come out from the water, it is fit for ploughing. Moreover, do thou come to the field with corn, for we will begin the ploughing in the morrow morning.' Thus said he to him; and his younger brother did all things as his elder brother had spoken unto him to do them.

And when the morn was come, they went to the fields with their things; and their hearts were pleased exceedingly with their task in the beginning of their work. And it came to pass after this that as they were in the field they stopped for corn, and he sent his younger brother, saying, 'Haste thou, bring to us corn from the farm.' And the younger brother found the wife of his elder brother, as she was sitting tying her hair. He said to her, 'Get up, and give to me corn, that I may run to the field, for my elder brother hastened me; do not delay.' She said to him, 'Go, open the bin, and thou shalt take to thyself according to thy will, that I may not drop my locks of hair while I dress them.'

The youth went into the stable; he took a large measure, for he desired to take much corn; he loaded it with wheat and barley; and he went out carrying it. She said to him, 'How much of the corn that is wanted, is that which is on thy shoulder?' He said to her, 'Three bushels of barley, and two of wheat, in all five; these are what are upon my shoulder:' thus said he to her. And she conversed with him, saying, 'There is great strength in thee, for I see thy might every day.' And her heart knew him with the knowledge of youth. And she arose and came to him, and conversed with him, saying, 'Come, stay with me, and it shall be well for thee, and I will make for thee beautiful garments.' Then the youth became like a panther of the south with fury at the evil speech which she had made to him; and she feared greatly. And he spake unto her, saying, 'Behold thou art to me as a mother, thy husband is to me as a father, for he who is elder than I has brought me up. What is this wickedness that thou hast said to me? Say it not to me again. For I will not tell it to any man, for I will not let it be uttered by the mouth of any man.' He lifted up his burden, and he went to the field and came to his elder brother; and they took up their work, to labour at their task.

Now afterward, at eventime, his elder brother was returning to his house; and the younger brother was following after his oxen, and he loaded himself with all the things of the field; and he brought his oxen before him, to make them lie down in their stable which was in the farm. And behold the wife of the elder brother was afraid for the words which she had said. She took a parcel of fat, she became like one who is evilly beaten, desiring to say to her husband, 'It is thy younger brother who has done this wrong.' Her husband returned in the even, as was his wont of every day; he came unto his house; he found his wife ill of violence; she did not give him water upon his hands as he used to have, she did not make a light before him, his house was in darkness, and she was lying very sick. Her husband said to her, 'Who has spoken with thee?'

Behold she said, 'No one has spoken with me except thy younger brother. When he came to take for thee corn he found me sitting alone; he said to me, "Come, let us stay together, tie up thy hair;" thus spake he to me. I did not listen to him, but thus spake I to him: "Behold, am I not thy mother, is not thy elder brother to thee as a father?" And he feared, and he beat me to stop me from making report to thee, and if thou lettest him live I shall die. Now behold he is coming in the evening; and I complain of these wicked words, for he would have done this even in daylight.'

And the elder brother became as a panther of the south; he sharpened his knife; he took it in his hand; he stood behind the door of his stable to slay his younger brother as he came in the evening to bring his cattle into the stable.

Now the sun went down, and he loaded himself with herbs in his daily manner. He came, and his foremost cow entered the stable, and she said to her keeper, 'Behold thou thy elder brother standing before thee with his knife to slay thee; flee from before him.' He heard what his first cow had said; and the next entering, she also said likewise. He looked beneath the door of the stable; he saw the feet of his elder brother; he was standing behind the door, and his knife was in his hand. He cast down his load to the ground, and betook himself to flee swiftly; and his elder brother pursued after him with his knife. Then the younger brother cried out unto Ra Harakhti, saying, 'My good Lord! Thou art he who divides the evil from the good.' And Ra stood and heard all his cry; and Ra made a wide water between him and his elder brother, and it was full of crocodiles; and the one brother was on one bank, and the other on the other bank; and the elder brother smote twice on his hands at not slaying him. Thus did he. And the younger brother called to the elder on the bank, saying, 'Stand still until the dawn of day; and when Ra ariseth, I shall judge with thee before Him, and He discerneth between the good and the evil. For I shall not be with thee any more for ever; I shall not be in the place in which thou art; I shall go to the valley of the acacia.'

Now when the land was lightened, and the next day appeared, Ra Harakhti arose, and one looked unto the other. And the youth spake with his elder brother, saying, 'Wherefore earnest thou after me to slay me in craftiness, when thou didst not hear the words of my mouth? For I am thy brother in truth, and thou art to me as a father, and thy wife even as a mother: is it not so? Verily, when I was sent to bring for us corn, thy wife said to me, "Come, stay with me;" for behold this has been turned over unto thee into another wise.' And he caused him to understand of all that happened with him and his wife. And he swore an oath by Ra Harakhti, saying, 'Thy coming to slay me by deceit with thy knife was an abomination.' Then the youth took a knife, and cut off of his flesh, and cast it into the water, and the fish swallowed it. He failed; he became faint; and his elder brother cursed his own heart greatly; he stood weeping for him afar off; he knew not how to pass over to where his younger brother was, because of the crocodiles. And the younger brother called unto him, saying, 'Whereas thou hast devised an evil thing, wilt thou not also devise a good thing, even like that which I would do unto thee? When thou goest to thy house thou must look to thy cattle, for I shall not stay in the place where thou art; I am going to the valley of the acacia. And now as to what thou shalt do for me; it is even that thou shalt come to seek after me, if thou perceivest a matter, namely, that there are things happening unto me. And this is what shall come to pass, that I shall draw out my soul, and I shall put it upon the top of the flowers of the acacia, and when the acacia is cut down, and it falls to the ground, and thou comest to seek for it, if thou searchest for it seven years do not let thy heart be wearied. For thou wilt find it, and thou must put it in a cup of cold water, and expect that I shall live again, that I may make answer to what has been done wrong.. And thou shalt know of this, that is to say, that things are happening to me, when one shall give to thee a cup of beer in thy hand, and it shall be troubled; stay not then, for verily it shall come to pass with thee.'

And the youth went to the valley of the acacia; and his elder brother went unto his house; his hand was laid on his head, and he cast dust on his head; he came to his house, and he slew his wife, he cast her to the dogs, and he sat in mourning for his younger brother.

Now many days after these things, the younger brother was in the valley of the acacia; there was none with him; he spent his time in hunting the beasts of the desert, and he came back in the even to lie down under the acacia, which bore his soul upon the topmost flower. And after this he built himself a tower with his own hands, in the valley of the acacia; it was full of all good things, that he might provide for himself a home.

And he went out from his tower, and he met the Nine Gods, who were walking forth to look upon the whole land. The Nine Gods talked one with another, and they said unto him, 'Ho! Bata, bull of the Nine Gods, art thou remaining alone? Thou hast left thy village for the wife of Anpu, thy elder brother. Behold his wife is slain. Thou hast given him an answer to all that was transgressed against thee.' And their hearts were vexed for him exceedingly. And Ra Harakhti said to Khnumu, 'Behold, frame thou a woman for Bata, that he may not remain alive alone.' And Khnumu made for him a mate to dwell with him. She was more beautiful in her limbs than any woman who is in the whole land. The essence of every god was in her. The seven Hathors came to see her: they said with one mouth, 'She will die a sharp death.'

And Bata loved her very exceedingly, and she dwelt in his house; he passed his time in hunting the beasts of the desert, and brought and laid them before her. He said, 'Go not outside, lest the sea seize thee; for I cannot rescue thee from it, for I am a woman like thee; my soul is placed on the head of the flower of the acacia; and if another find it, I must fight with him.' And he opened unto her his heart in all its nature.

Now after these things Bata went to hunt in his daily manner. And the young girl went to walk under the acacia which was by the side of her house. Then the sea saw her, and cast its waves up after her. She betook herself to flee from before it. She entered her house. And the sea called unto the acacia, saying, 'Oh, would that I could seize her!' And the acacia brought a lock from her hair, and the sea carried it to Egypt, and dropped it in the place of the fullers of Pharaoh's linen. The smell of the lock of hair entered into the clothes of Pharaoh; and they were wroth with the fullers of Pharaoh, saying, 'The smell of ointment is in the clothes of Pharaoh.' And the people were rebuked every day, they knew not what they should do. And the chief fuller of Pharaoh walked by the bank, and his heart was very evil within him after the daily quarrel with him. He stood still, he stood upon the sand opposite to the lock of hair, which was in the water, and he made one enter into the water and bring it to him; and there was found in it a smell, exceeding sweet. He took it to Pharaoh; and they brought the scribes and the wise men, and they said unto Pharaoh, 'This lock of hair belongs to a daughter of Ra Harakhti: the essence of every god is in her, and it is a tribute to thee from another land.

Let messengers go to every strange land to seek her: and as for the messenger who shall go to the valley of the acacia, let many men go with him to bring her.' Then said his majesty, 'Excellent exceedingly is what has been said to us;' and they sent them. And many days after these things the people who were sent to strange lands came to give report unto the king: but there came not those who went to the valley of the acacia, for Bata had slain them, but let one of them return to give a report to the king. His majesty sent many men and soldiers, as well as horsemen, to bring her back. And there was a woman amongst them, and to her had been given in her hand beautiful ornaments of a woman. And the girl came back with her, and they rejoiced over her in the whole land.

And his majesty loved her exceedingly, and raised her to high estate; and he spake unto her that she should tell him concerning her husband. And she said, 'Let the acacia be cut down, and let one chop it up.' And they sent men and soldiers with their weapons to cut down the acacia; and they came to the acacia, and they cut the flower upon which was the soul of Bata, and he fell dead suddenly.

And when the next day came, and the earth was lightened, the acacia was cut down. And Anpu, the elder brother of Bata, entered his house, and washed his hands; and one gave him a cup of beer, and it became troubled; and one gave him another of wine, and the smell of it was evil. Then he took his staff, and his sandals, and likewise his clothes, with his weapons of war; and he betook himself forth to the valley of the acacia. He entered the tower of his younger brother, and he found him lying upon his mat; he was dead. And he wept when he saw his younger brother verily lying dead. And he went out to seek the soul of his younger brother under the acacia tree, under which his younger brother lay in the evening. He spent three years in seeking for it, but found it not. And when he began the fourth year, he desired in his heart to return into Egypt; he said 'I will go to-morrow morn:' thus spake he in his heart.

Now when the land lightened, and the next day appeared, he was walking under the acacia; he was spending his time in seeking it. And he returned in the evening, and laboured at seeking it again. He found a seed. He returned with it. Behold this was the soul of his younger brother. He brought a cup of cold water, and he cast the seed into it: and he sat down, as he was wont. Now when the night came his soul sucked up the water; Bata shuddered in all his limbs, and he looked on his elder brother; his soul was in the cup. Then Anpu took the cup of cold water, in which the soul of his younger brother was; Bata drank it, his soul stood again in its place, and he became as he had been. They embraced each other, and they conversed together.

And Bata said to his elder brother, 'Behold I am to become as a great bull, which bears every good mark; no one knoweth its history, and thou must sit upon my back. When the sun arises I shall be in the place where my wife is, that I may return answer to her; and thou must take me to the place where the king is. For all good things shall be done for thee; for one shall lade thee with silver and gold, because thou bringest me to Pharaoh, for I become a great marvel, and they shall rejoice for me in all the land. And thou shalt go to thy village.'

And when the land was lightened, and the next day appeared, Bata became in the form which he had told to his elder brother. And Anpu sat upon his back until the dawn. He came to the place where the king was, and they made his majesty to know of him; he saw him, and he was exceeding joyful with him. He made for him great offerings, saying, 'This is a great wonder which has come to pass.' There were rejoicings over him in the whole land. They presented unto him silver and gold for his elder brother, who went and stayed in his village. They gave to the bull many men and many things, and Pharaoh loved him exceedingly above all that is in this land.

And after many days after these things, the bull entered the purified place; he stood in the place where the princess was; he began to speak with her, saying, 'Behold, I am alive indeed.' And she said to him, 'And, pray, who art thou?' He said to her, 'I am Bata. I perceived when thou causedst that they should destroy the acacia of Pharaoh, which was my abode, that I might not be suffered to live. Behold, I am alive indeed, I am as an ox.' Then the princess feared exceedingly for the words that her husband had spoken to her. And he went out from the purified place.

And his majesty was sitting, making a good day with her: she was at the table of his majesty, and the king was exceeding pleased with her. And she said to his majesty, 'Swear to me by God, saying, "What thou shalt say, I will obey it for thy sake."' He hearkened unto all that she said, even this. 'Let me eat of the liver of the ox, because he is fit for nought:' thus spake she to him. And the king was exceeding sad at her words, the heart of Pharaoh grieved him greatly. And after the land was lightened, and the next day appeared, they proclaimed a great feast with offerings to the ox. And the king sent one of the chief butchers of his majesty, to cause the ox to be sacrificed. And when he was sacrificed, as he was upon the shoulders of the people, he shook his neck, and he threw two drops of blood over against the two doors of his majesty. The one fell upon the one side, on the great door of Pharaoh, and the other upon the other door. They grew as two great Persea trees, and each of them was excellent.

And one went to tell unto his majesty, 'Two great Persea trees have grown, as a great marvel of his majesty, in the night by the side of the great gate of his majesty.' And there was rejoicing for them in all the land, and there were offerings made to them.

And when the days were multiplied after these things, his majesty was adorned with the blue crown, with garlands of flowers on his neck, and he was upon the chariot of pale gold, and he went out from the palace to behold the Persea trees: the princess also was going out with horses behind his majesty. And his majesty sat beneath one of the Persea trees, and it spake thus with his wife: 'Oh thou deceitful one, I am Bata, I am alive, though I have been evilly entreated. I knew who caused the acacia to be cut down by Pharaoh at my dwelling. I then became an ox, and thou causedst that I should be killed.'

And many days after these things the princess stood at the table of Pharaoh, and the king was pleased with her. And she said to his majesty, 'Swear to me by God, saying, "That which the princess shall say to me I will obey it for her."' And he hearkened unto all she said. And he commanded, 'Let these two Persea trees be cut down, and let them be made into goodly planks.' And he hearkened unto all she said. And after this his majesty sent skilful craftsmen, and they cut down the Persea trees of Pharaoh; and the princess, the royal wife, was standing looking on, and they did all that was in her heart unto the trees. But a chip flew up, and it entered into the mouth of the princess; she swallowed it, and after many days she bore a son. And one went to tell his majesty, 'There is born to thee a son.' And they brought him, and gave to him a nurse and servants; and there were rejoicings in the whole land. And the king sat making a merry day, as they were about the naming of him, and his majesty loved him exceedingly at that moment, and the king raised him to be the royal son of Kush.

Now after the days had multiplied after these things, his majesty made him heir of all the land. And many days after that, when he had fulfilled many years as heir, his majesty flew up to heaven. And the heir said, 'Let my great nobles of his majesty be brought before me, that I may make them to know all that has happened to me.' And they brought also before him his wife, and he judged with her before him, and they agreed with him. They brought to him his elder brother; he made him hereditary prince in all his land. He was thirty years king of Egypt, and he died, and his elder brother stood in his place on the day of burial.

Excellently finished in peace, for the ka of the scribe of the treasury Kagabu, of the treasury of Pharaoh, and for the scribe Hora, and the scribe Meremapt. Written by the scribe Anena, the owner of this roll. He who speaks against this roll, may Tahuti smite him.

THE DOOMED PRINCE

Edited by W. M. Flinders Petrie

This tale is preserved in one of the Harris papyri (No. 500) in the British Museum. It has been translated by Goodwin, Chabas, Maspero, and Ebers. The present version is adapted from that of Maspero, with frequent reference by Mr Griffith to the original. There is here a new element, that of striving and of unrest, quite foreign to the old Egyptian mind. The age of this tale is shown plainly in the incidents. The prince goes to the chief of Naharaina, a land probably unknown to the Egyptians until the Asiatic conquests of the XVIIIth Dynasty had led them to the upper waters of the Euphrates. In earlier days Sanehat fled to the frontier at the Wady Tumilat, and was quite lost to Egypt when he settled in the south of Palestine. But when the Doomed Prince goes out of Egypt he goes to the chief of Naharaina, as the frontier State. This stamps the tale as subsequent to the wars of the Tahutimes family, and reflects rather the peaceful intercourse of the great monarch Amenhotep III.

There once was a king to whom no son was born; and his heart was grieved, and he prayed for himself unto the gods around him for a child. They decreed that one should be born to him. And his wife, after her time was fulfilled, brought forth a son. Then came the Hathors to decree for him a destiny; they said, 'His death is to be by the crocodile, or by the serpent, or by the dog.' Then the people who stood by heard this, and they went to tell it to his majesty. Then his majesty's heart sickened very greatly. And his majesty caused a house to be built upon the desert; it was furnished with people and with all good things of the royal house, that the child should not go abroad. And when the child was grown, he went up upon the roof, and he saw a dog; it was following a man who was walking on the road. He spoke to his page, who was with him, 'What is this that walks behind the man who is coming along the road?' He answered him, 'This is a dog.' The child said to him, 'Let there be brought to me one like it.' The page went to repeat it to his majesty. And his majesty said, 'Let there be brought to him a little pet dog, lest his heart be sad.' And behold they brought to him the dog.

Then when the days increased after this, and when the child became grown in all his limbs, he sent a message to his father saying, 'Come, wherefore am I kept here? Inasmuch as I am fated to three evil fates, let me follow my desire. Let God do what is in His heart.' They agreed to all he said, and gave him all sorts of arms, and also his dog to follow him, and they took him to the east country, and said to him, 'Behold, go thou whither thou wilt.' His dog was with him, and he went northward, following his heart in the desert, while he lived on all the best of the game of the desert. He went to the chief of Naharaina.

And behold there had not been any born to the chief of Naharaina, except one daughter. Behold, there had been built for her a house; its seventy windows were seventy cubits from the ground. And the chief caused to be brought all the sons of the chiefs of the land of Khalu, and said to them, 'He who reaches the window of my daughter, she shall be to him for a wife.'

And many days after these things, as they were in their daily task, the youth rode by the place where they were. They took the youth to their house, they bathed him, they gave provender to his horses, they brought all kinds of things for the youth, they perfumed him, they anointed his feet, they gave him portions of their own food; and they spake to him, 'Whence comest thou, goodly youth?' He said to them, 'I am son of an officer of the land of Egypt; my mother is dead, and my father has taken another wife. And when she bore children, she grew to hate me, and I have come as a fugitive from before her.' And they embraced him, and kissed him.

And after many days were passed, he said to the youths, 'What is it that ye do here?' And they said to him, 'We spend our time in this: we climb up, and he who shall reach the window of the daughter of the chief of Naharaina, to him will he given her to wife.' He said to them, 'If it please you, let me behold the matter, that I may come to climb with you.' They went to climb, as was their daily wont: and the youth stood afar off to behold; and the face of the daughter of the chief of Naharaina was turned to them.

And another day the sons came to climb, and the youth came to climb with the sons of the chiefs. He climbed, and he reached the window of the daughter of the chief of Naharaina. She kissed him, she embraced him in all his limbs.

And one went to rejoice the heart of her father, and said to him, 'One of the people has reached the window of thy daughter.' And the prince inquired of the messenger, saying, 'The son of which of the princes is it?' And he replied to him, 'It is the son of an officer, who has come as a fugitive from the land of Egypt, fleeing from before his stepmother when she had children.' Then the chief of Naharaina was exceeding angry; and he said, 'Shall I indeed give my daughter to the Egyptian fugitive? Let him go back whence he came.' And one came to tell the youth, 'Go back to the place thou earnest from.' But the maiden seized his hand; she swore an oath by God, saying, 'By the being of Ra Harakhti, if one takes him from me, I will not eat, I will not drink, I shall die in that same hour.' The messenger went to tell unto her father all that she said. Then the prince sent men to slay the youth, while he was in his house. But the maiden said, 'By the being of Ra, if one slay him I shall be dead ere the sun goeth down. I will not pass an hour of life if I am parted from him.' And one went to tell her father. Then the prince made them bring the youth with the maiden. The youth was seized with fear when he came before the prince. But he embraced him, he kissed him all over, and said, 'Oh! tell me who thou art; behold, thou art to me as a son.' He said to him, 'I am a son of an officer of the land of Egypt; my mother died, my father took to him a second wife; she came to hate me, and I fled a fugitive from before her.' He then gave to him his daughter to wife; he gave also to him a house, and serfs, and fields, also cattle and all manner of good things.

But after the days of these things were passed, the youth said to his wife, 'I am doomed to three fates – a crocodile, a serpent, and a dog.' She said to him, 'Let one kill the dog which belongs to thee.' He replied to her, 'I am not going to kill my dog, which I have brought up from when it was small.' And she feared greatly for her husband, and would not let him go alone abroad.

And one went with the youth toward the land of Egypt, to travel in that country. Behold the crocodile of the river, he came out by the town in which the youth was. And in that town was a mighty man. And the mighty man would not suffer the crocodile to escape. And when the crocodile was bound, the mighty man went out and walked abroad. And when the sun rose the mighty man went back to the house; and he did so every day, during two months of days.

Now when the days passed after this, the youth sat making a good day in his house. And when the evening came he lay down on his bed, sleep seized upon his limbs; and his wife filled a bowl of milk, and placed it by his side. Then came out a serpent from his hole, to bite the youth; behold his wife was sitting by him, she lay not down. Thereupon the servants gave milk to the serpent, and he drank, and was drunk, and lay upside down. Then his wife made it to perish with the blows of her dagger. And they woke her husband, who was astonished; and she said unto him, 'Behold thy God has given one of thy dooms into thy hand; He will also give thee the others.' And he sacrificed to God, adoring Him, and praising His spirits from day to day.

And when the days were passed after these things, the youth went to walk in the fields of his domain. He went not alone, behold his dog was following him. And his dog ran aside after the wild game, and he followed the dog. He came to the river, and entered the river behind his dog. Then came out the crocodile, and took him to the place where the mighty man was. And the crocodile said to the youth, 'I am thy doom, following after thee. ...'

[Here the papyrus breaks off.]

THE STORY OF THE SHIPWRECKED SAILOR

Translated by W. M. Flinders Petrie

This tale is only known in one copy, preserved in the
Hermitage collection at St Petersburg. Two translations
of it have appeared by M. Golenischeff. The tale is that of
a returned sailor, speaking to his superior and telling his
adventures, to induce him to send him on with an introduction
to the king. At first his master professes to disbelieve him,
and then the sailor protests that this happened to himself,
and gives his narrative. The idea of an enchanted island,
which has risen from the waves and will sink again, is here
found to be one of the oldest plots for a tale of marvels. But
the construction is far more advanced than that of the tales
of the magicians. The family of serpents and the manner of
the great serpent is well conceived, and there are many fine
touches of literary quality: such as noise as of thunder, the
trees shaking and the earth being moved at the appearance

of the great serpent – the speeches of the serpent and his threat – the sailors who had seen heaven and earth – the contempt of the serpent for his offerings. The colophon of the copyist at the end shows by the style of the name that it belongs to the earlier part of the XIIth Dynasty, and if so, the composition might be referred to the opening of foreign trade under Sankhkara or Amenemhat I.

The wise servant said, 'Let thy heart be satisfied, O my lord, for that we have come back to the country; after we have long been on board, and rowed much, the prow has at last touched land. All the people rejoice, and embrace us one after another. Moreover, we have come back in good health, and not a man is lacking; although we have been to the ends of Wawat, and gone through the land of Senmut, we have returned in peace, and our land – behold, we have come back to it. Hear me, my lord; I have no other refuge. Wash thee, and turn the water over thy ringers; then go and tell the tale to the majesty.' His lord replied, 'Thy heart continues still its wandering words! but although the mouth of a man may save him, his words may also cover his face with confusion. Wilt thou do then as thy heart moves thee? This that thou wilt say, tell quietly.' The sailor then answered, 'Now I shall tell that which has happened to me, to my very self I was going to the mines of Pharaoh, and I went down on the sea on a ship of 150 cubits long and 40 cubits wide, with 150 sailors of the best of Egypt, who had seen heaven and earth, and whose hearts were stronger than lions. They had said that the wind would not be contrary, or that there would be none. But as we approached the land the wind arose, and threw up waves eight cubits high. As for me, I seized a piece of wood; but those who were in the vessel perished, without one remaining. A wave threw me on an island, after that I had been three days alone, without a companion beside my own heart. I laid me in a thicket, and the shadow covered me. Then stretched I my limbs to try to find something for my mouth. I found there figs and grapes, all manner of good herbs, berries and grain, melons of all kinds, fishes and birds. Nothing was lacking. And I satisfied myself; and left on the ground that which was over, of what my arms had been filled withal. I dug a pit, I lighted a fire, and I made a burnt-offering unto the gods. Suddenly I heard a noise as of thunder, which I thought to be that of a wave of the sea. The trees shook, and the earth was moved. I uncovered my face, and I saw that a serpent drew near. He was thirty cubits long, and his beard greater than two cubits; his body was as overlayed with gold, and his colour as that of true lazuli. He coiled himself before me. Then he opened his mouth, while that I lay on my face before him, and he said to me, "What has brought thee, what has brought thee, little one, what has brought thee? If thou sayest not speedily what has brought thee to this isle, I will make thee know thyself; as a flame thou shalt vanish, if thou tellest me not something I have not heard, or which I knew not, before thee." Then he took me in his mouth and carried me to his resting-place, and layed me down without any hurt. I was whole and sound, and nothing was gone from me. Then he opened his mouth against me, while that I lay on my face before him, and he said, "What has

251

brought thee, what has brought thee, little one, what has brought thee to this isle which is in the sea, and of which the shores are in the midst of the waves?" Then I replied to him, and holding my arms low before him, I said to him, "I was embarked for the mines by the order of the majesty, in a ship, 150 cubits was its length, and the width of it 40 cubits. It had 150 sailors of the best of Egypt, who had seen heaven and earth, and the hearts of whom were stronger than lions. They said that the wind would not be contrary, or that there would be none. Each of them exceeded his companion in the prudence of his heart and the strength of his arm, and I was not beneath any of them. A storm came upon us while we were on the sea. Hardly could we reach to the shore when the wind waxed yet greater, and the waves rose even eight cubits. As for me, I seized a piece of wood, while those who were in the boat perished without one being left with me for three days. Behold me now before thee, for I was brought to this isle by a wave of the sea." Then said he to me, "Fear not, fear not, little one, and make not thy face sad. If thou hast come to me, it is God who has let thee live. For it is He who has brought thee to this isle of the blest, where nothing is lacking, and which is filled with all good after another, until thou shalt be four months in this isle. Then a ship shall come from thy land with sailors, and thou shalt leave with them and go to thy country, and thou shalt die in thy town." Converse is pleasing, and he who tastes of it passes over his misery. I will therefore tell thee of that which is in this isle. I am here with my brethren and my children around me; we are seventy-five serpents, children, and kindred; without naming a young girl who was brought unto me by chance, and on whom the fire of heaven fell, and burnt her to ashes. As for thee if thou art strong, and if thy heart waits patiently, thou shalt press thy infants to thy bosom and embrace thy wife. Thou shalt return to thy house which is full of all good things, thou shalt see thy land, where thou shalt dwell in the midst of thy kindred." Then I bowed, in my obeisance, and I touched the ground before him. "Behold now that which I have told thee before. I shall tell of thy presence unto Pharaoh, I shall make him to know of thy greatness, and I will bring to thee of the sacred oils and perfumes, and of incense of the temples with which all gods are honoured. I shall tell, moreover, of that which I do now see (thanks to him), and there shall be rendered to thee praises before the fulness of all the land. I shall slay asses for thee in sacrifice, I shall pluck for thee the birds, and I shall bring for thee ships full of all kinds of the treasures of Egypt, as is comely to do unto a god, a friend of men in a far country, of which men know not." Then he smiled at my speech, because of that which was in his heart, for he said to me, "Thou art not rich in perfumes, for all that thou hast is but common incense. As for me I am prince of the land of Punt, and I have perfumes. Only the oil which thou sayedst thou wouldest bring is not common in this isle. But, when thou shalt depart from this place, thou shalt never more see this isle; it shall be changed into waves." And, behold, when the ship drew near, according to all that he had told me before, I got me up into an high tree, to strive to see those who were within it. Then I came and told to him this matter; but it was already known unto him before. Then he said to me,

"Farewell, farewell, go to thy house, little one, see again thy children, and let thy name be good in thy town; these are my wishes for thee." Then I bowed myself before him, and held my arms low before him, and he, he gave me gifts of precious perfumes, of cassia, of sweet woods, of kohl, of cypress, an abundance of incense, of ivory tusks, of baboons, of apes, and all kind of precious things. I embarked all in the ship which was come, and bowing myself, I prayed God for him. Then he said to me, "Behold thou shalt come to thy country in two months, thou shalt press to thy bosom thy children, and thou shalt rest in thy tomb." After this I went down to the shore unto the ship, and I called to the sailors who were there. Then on the shore I rendered adoration to the master of this isle and to those who dwelt therein. When we shall come, in our return, to the house of Pharaoh, in the second month, according to all that the serpent has said, we shall approach unto the palace. And I shall go in before Pharaoh, I shall bring the gifts which I have brought from this isle into the country. Then he shall thank me before the fulness of all the land. Grant then unto me a follower, and lead me to the courtiers of the king. Cast thy eye upon me, after that I am come to land again, after that I have both seen and proved this. Hear my prayer, for it is good to listen to people. It was said unto me, "Become a wise man, and thou shalt come to honour," and behold I have become such.'

This is finished from its beginning unto its end, even as it was found in a writing. It is written by the scribe of cunning fingers Ameni-amen-aa; may he live in life, wealth, and health!